STRIKE FORCE

U.S. MARINE CORPS SPECIAL OPERATIONS

PHOTOGRAPHY AND TEXT BY AGOSTINO VON HASSELL

"Chesty," the Marine Corps mascot, appears in the insignia on this UH-1 Huey helicopter.

Designed by Marilyn F. Appleby.
Edited by Kathleen D. Valenzi.
Photographs and text copyright © 1991 by Agostino von Hassell, all rights reserved.

Library of Congress Catalog Card Number 90-84685
ISBN 0-943231-38-8

Published by Howell Press Inc., 1147 River Road, Bay 2, Charlottesville, Virginia 22901. Telephone (804) 977-4006.

Printed and bound in Singapore by Tien Wah Press.

Second printing

HOWELL PRESS

DEDICATED TO THE MARINES OF THE 26TH MEU (SOC); 2ND BN, 8TH MAR; HMM-264 "THE BLACK KNIGHTS"; AND MSSG-26.

Many Marines helped to make this book a reality. To thank and honor them and their Corps, which takes pride in taking care of its own, part of the proceeds of the sale of this book are being donated to the Marine Corps Scholarship Foundation.

(Above) Flight operations resume at dawn as AV-8B Harriers return to the USS *Nassau* somewhere in the Mediterranean Sea. A Marine Expeditionary Unit typically has its own complement of six Harriers. (Facing) A Marine sews up his torn trousers.

CONTENTS

PREFACE
EAGLE, GLOBE AND ANCHOR

INTEGRATING AIR POWER with ground assault forces is a U.S. Marine Corps tradition. To this day the Corps remains unique as a service by combining these essential combat elements in one uniform. Much envied by others, this integration has never been copied, and the Corps is improving it.

Today's U.S. Marine Corps is enhancing deployed units with special-operations capabilities. In providing this training, the Marine Corps feels some urgency. Proud to be the "first to fight," Marines throughout history have entered battles at a moment's notice, as happened during the invasion of Grenada when the Marine Corps had just a few days' advance warning, or in 1990 when 50,000 Marines deployed to Saudi Arabia in less than two weeks. In the early 1990s, the Corps numbers few active-duty Marines who are combat veterans, men like Gunnery Sergeant Dan Daly, who at Belleau Wood, France, in June 1918 swung his rifle and urged his untested troops on with a resounding, "Come on you sons of bitches; do you want to live forever?" But they are as mentally prepared as their predecessors.

To the uninitiated the term "special operations" may call to mind images of fast-spinning action familiar from TV shows or hit movies, but special-operations-capable Marines are nothing like "Rambo."

Becoming special-operations capable means performing often-dry staff work, attending endless briefings, devoting long hours to assigned tasks, giving mind-boggling attention to detail, and training intensively to acquire a diversity of skills in a surprisingly short period of time.

In the Pacific Ocean and the Mediterranean Sea (the "Med") are now deployed modern Marine Corps units that have recently acquired special-operations capabilities in addition to their conventional amphibious skills. This book focuses on one of them, the 26th Marine Expeditionary Unit. For almost a year, I became part of that group, participating in six months of exhausting predeployment training and a five-and-half-month deployment to the Med.

While my primary goal is to depict their special-operations capabilities, innovative techniques, and state-of-the-art equipment and electronics, I also want to show the people at the heart of it all, the Marines who make it work, including the Corps' innovative leaders. Nothing throughout the colorful history of the Corps has been more vital to its success than excellence in leadership.

The spirit of the young Marine remains unchanged, expressed in that characteristic swagger when on liberty and that irrepressible pride when talking with outsiders. As "Soldiers of the Sea," today's Marines can storm ashore with the same fiery fury seen at Guadalcanal, Tarawa, Saipan, and Iwo Jima during World War II. To borrow a slogan from the Italian Marines: "It is better to be a lion for a day, than to be a sheep for a hundred years."

A USMC amphibious assault can come from far over the horizon on an unsuspecting foe. Marine forces can conduct landing operations at night, in foul weather, and under complete radio silence in order to heighten the surprise of their attack. Here a platoon commander rides an Amtrac to the beach.

ARCHIVAL
USMC SPECIAL MISSIONS

U.S. MARINES have operated in the shadowy world of low-intensity conflicts and special operations since as early as 1801-1807 in the "war" against the Barbary Pirates. Less well known is the Marine Corps' role in what was the first documented "hostage rescue," the raid on Harpers Ferry, Virginia, in 1859.

In the long years between the end of the Civil War and the First World War, Marines were called upon for many specialized missions; the term "special operations" hadn't been coined yet. For instance, in 1866 Marine troops aboard a Navy vessel helped stop a mutiny on a mail ship in the Caribbean, and in 1882 U.S. Marines along with Royal Marines landed in Alexandria, Egypt, to stop looting, arson, and riots. To put down a secessionist rebellion in 1885, the Marine Corps and Navy were ordered into Panama to protect American lives and property. According to Marine Corps records, Marines landed on foreign shores 24 times between 1866 and 1889 to guard American interests.

From 1889 to 1914 the use of Marine forces picked up as America's worldwide interests began to expand more rapidly. Marine forces raided an installation in Cuba in 1898, destroying cable houses and capturing a vital lighthouse. Another celebrated effort was the defense of the Peking Legations during the Boxer Rebellion in 1900. From 1889 until 1914, Marine forces intervened about 100 times abroad, including instances when Marines landed in Nicaragua (1899, 1910, and 1912), Panama (1901, 1902, 1903), Honduras (1903), the Dominican Republic (1903, 1912-1924), Cuba (1906, 1912), Mexico (1914), and Haiti (1914-1918) to quell disturbances or help stabilize friendly regimes.

The pattern continued between the two World Wars, with Marines being called upon to protect civilians or conduct special missions. Knowledge of small conflicts gained by Marines in the Nicaraguan "Banana War" and through protection of the Legation Quarters in Shanghai found its way into the new organizations established during World War II.

To give the Marine Corps a special raid-force capability, special-operations battalions (as they would be called today) were formed. The two men most responsible for this movement were Lieutenant Colonel Merritt A. "Red Mike" Edson, who spent many years in China and formed the 1st Raider Battalion, and Lieutenant Colonel Evans F. Carlson, who formed the 2nd Raider Battalion, whose small unit, special warfare techniques were inspired by Chinese communist warfare, a topic Colonel Carlson had studied while stationed in Shanghai in the 1930s. Colonel Carlson's force contributed much to the body of knowledge on small actions and raids and added "Gung-Ho," the Chinese term for working together, to the Marine Corps vocabulary.

The Raider Battalions, which served as a strike force for specialized operations throughout the war in the Pacific, were later merged into the Fourth Marine Regiment. In a sense they were dissolved, because Marine Corps leadership viewed with some concern these specialized units and objected to maintaining "an elite force within an elite fighting force." That experience, more than anything else, helped shape the Corps' approach to special operations today.

The lessons learned by the Raider Battalions were picked up by numerous Marine units during Vietnam and, in particular, by Force Reconnaissance Units that conducted a variety of special operations during the Asian conflict.

The Marine Corps has been in the business of special operations continuously for almost 200 years. Terminology may have changed through time, but not the missions that Marines have been called on to undertake.

Apart from Vietnam and Korea, Marine forces have been used repeatedly since the end of World War II for missions now best described by the term "special operations." These include the 1958 landing of a Marine peace-keeping force in Beirut to protect American interests, and the evacuation of 1,750 Americans from the U.S. Embassy in Santo Domingo, Dominican Republic, in 1965. The latter action was conducted in part by HMM-264, the Black Knights squadron, and was the first ever all-helicopter night-time operation of its kind.

In 1988 the first Marine unit carrying the Special Operations Capable (SOC) designation was active in combat, this time in the Persian Gulf, taking out Iranian oil rigs and landing on suspected minelaying ships. In 1989 Marines were once again stationed off Beirut following threats by extremists to execute American hostages. In 1990 Marines not only invaded Panama, where Panamanian dictator Manuel Noriega, a known drug kingpin, had publicly threatened American lives, but they also found themselves evacuating American citizens in Liberia where civil unrest was brewing. Following Iraq's invasion of Saudi Arabia in 1990, the Corps deployed one complete Marine Expeditionary Force, the first such deployment since Vietnam. What the years ahead will bring is unknown, but one thing can be counted on: Marines, now possessing unique special-operations capabilities, will continue to successfully face any challenge and maintain the Corps' tradition of excellence in service.

(Top) Lt. Presley Neville O'Bannon, along with seven U.S. Marines and a large force of mercenaries, crossed the Barca desert on camel and toppled the regime of Bashaw Yusuf Karamanli of Tripoli in 1805. In gratitude, Marine Corps legend has it, the new Bashaw, Hamet Karamanli, gave Lt. O'Bannon a sword with a Mamelucke hilt, which became the model for the sword Marine officers carry today. (Bottom) "Burning of the Frigate PHILADELPHIA in the Harbor of Tripoli," February 16, 1804, artist unknown. After the PHILADELPHIA ran into a shoal off Tripoli Harbor in 1804, Bashaw Yusuf captured the frigate and took her crew prisoner. U.S. Navy Lt. Stephen Decatur led the raiding party that reboarded the frigate and set her ablaze to deny the Bashaw his war prize.

All archival photos courtesy the National Archives unless otherwise noted.

(Top) Marines helped ''show the flag'' during the famous landing of USN Commodore Matthew Calbraith Perry to meet the Imperial Commissioners at Yokohama, Japan, March 8, 1854. (Bottom) The USMC's first documented hostage rescue mission was conducted at Harper's Ferry, Virginia, by Marines dispatched from the Marine Barracks in Washington, D.C., in October 1859. This depiction, artist unknown, shows the interior of the engine house at Harper's Ferry during the attack by Marine forces. *(Print from Thunder at Harper's Ferry by Allan Keller)*

(Top) This Korean headquarters flag was captured at Fort McKee, Korea, by Pvt. Purvis of the USS ALASKA, assisted by Cpl. Brown of the USS COLORADO, during attacks by U.S. Marines on the Salee River Forts, June 10-11, 1871. Capt. McLane Tilton, commanding Marines, stands to the right of the Medal of Honor recipients. A subsequent report on the engagement bestowed on Capt. Tilton and his Marines ''the honor of the first landing and last leaving the shore, in leading the advance on the march, on entering the forts and in acting as skirmishers; chosen as the advanced guard on account of their steadiness and discipline, and looked to with confidence in case of difficulty, their whole behavior on the march and in the assault proved that it was not misplaced.'' (Center) Interior of Fort McKee, known as the Citadel, after its capture by U.S. Marines and Sailors. (Bottom) U.S. and Royal Marines at Alexandria, Egypt, 1882. Marine forces had been called in to quell local disturbances. Throughout U.S. Marine Corps history, peacekeeping and the protection of American interests has been a special mission of the Corps.

(Top) Colonel Robert W. Huntington, astride his horse in Cuba in 1898, was one of the most famous Marines of the Spanish-American War, particularly during the ''100 hours of fighting'' at Guantanamo Bay, where he ''made the greatest contribution to the Marine Corps' reputation for combat, valor, and readiness,'' according to Allan R. Millet in *Semper Fidelis: The History of the United States Marine Corps*. (Bottom) U.S. Marines take positions after one of their many landing operations in Guantanamo, Cuba, 1898.

(Top) During the 1900 Boxer Rebellion in Peking, China, U.S. Marines earned lasting fame in their defense of the Legations' Quarter. Historically, Marines have been responsible for protecting U.S. embassies and consulates. (Center) This view of a U.S. Marine bunker during the defense of the foreign legations was taken in Peking, China, 1900. (Bottom) The Allies celebrate their victory within the Forbidden City in Peking, China. Military units (in most cases Marines) from virtually all European nations participated in the action to liberate the foreign legations. U.S. Marines have served in multinational forces numerous times since then, including Beirut, Lebanon, in 1982-1984 and the Persian Gulf beginning in 1990.

(Top left) Rebel soldiers, driven into American lines by Mexican Federal Troops, are taken to Fort San Juan de Uloa by U.S. Marines in Vera Cruz, Mexico, August 10, 1914. (Top right) U.S. Marines traverse inhospitable terrain to round up Mexican rebels near Vera Cruz, 1914. (Center left) Gunfire from U.S. Navy ships is adjusted by Marines signaling from an exposed position on shore during the naval bombardment of Vera Cruz, Mexico, 1914. (Center right) Mascots, such as this dog ''serving'' with a Marine artillery landing detachment in 1914, have always accompanied Marines into action. (Bottom) On April 21, 1914, the first Marine landing party leaves the USS PRAIRIE for the shores of Vera Cruz, Mexico.

(Top) Marines patrol the Coca River in Nicaragua, 1927 or 1928. (Center) A USMC pack train in Nicaragua. The Nicaraguan campaigns of the 1920s and '30s were seminal events in Marine Corps history. Marines learned valuable lessons in fighting ''small wars,'' and many of these lessons were later incorporated into doctrine supporting missions, including special operations. The *Small Arms Manual*, first published in 1935, listed these experiences and has become a Marine Corps classic, which is studied diligently to this day and considered pertinent to the many challenges facing Marines in the 1990s. (Bottom) Left to right: Sgt. Owen, GySgt. Wilson, and Sgt. Robinson following contact with insurgents at La Palancer, Nicaragua, August 1928.

15

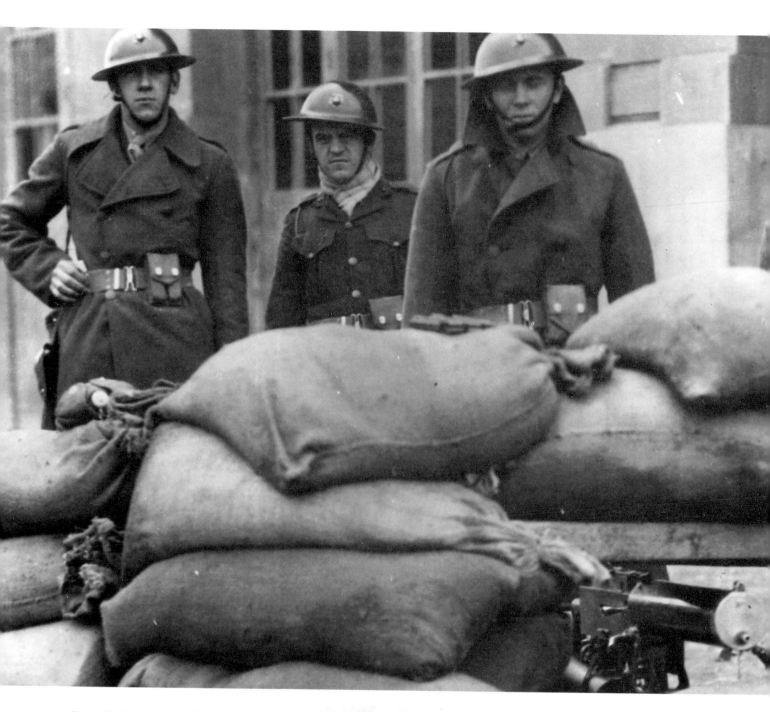

(Top) U.S. Marines of the 28th Company, 4th Marine Regiment, man a machine gun position at the Ichang Road Fire Station, Shanghai, China, on March 10, 1932. (Bottom) Camp Butler, Shanghai, China, 1927. For many years Marines of the 4th Marine Regiment, often referred to as "China Marines," guarded American interests in Shanghai. Two "China" Marines gained lasting fame in the difficult business of special operations: Lt. Col. Merrit A. ("Red Mike") Edson, who spent many years in China and later formed the 1st Raider Battalion, and Lt. Col. Evans F. Carlson, who was inspired by Chinese communists fighting a drawn-out guerilla war and formed the 2nd Raider Battalion.

(Top) Marines from transports and warships docked at Shanghai Harbor march through the streets of the International Settlement on April 1, 1927, in what was termed by government officials as an ''exercise march only'' and not an armed display to impress the Chinese in Shanghai. (Bottom) U.S. Marines with fixed bayonets take aim behind sand bag emplacements in Shanghai, China, on April 8, 1938.

(Top) Tulagi Island, part of the Solomon Island group east of New Guinea, burns in the distance after sea and aerial bombardments on August 7-9, 1942. (Bottom) U.S. Marines land on Tulagi Island in early August 1942. The 1st Parachute Battalion and 1st Raider Battalion had been assigned to this operation, which was the first major operation conducted by WWII Marine special operations forces.

(Top) U.S. Marine Raiders pose in front of a Japanese dugout at Cape Torokina on Bougainville after bloody fighting against Japanese troops, November 2, 1943. (Bottom left) During two days and nights of fierce jungle fighting on Bougainville, the Marine Raider Battalion repelled repeated attacks by strong Japanese forces against the Piva Trail roadblock, November 9, 1943. (Bottom right) 155mm guns of the First Marine Amphibious Corps are unloaded on the beach at Bougainville in late November 1943. Marine special forces—the Raider Battalions—partici-pated in the assault on the isle.

(Top left) Marine Staff Sgt. Thomas Gentile gets his first look at Lebanon through the porthole of his airplane. He was one of the first Marines to be airlifted into Beirut during a July 1958 peacekeeping mission. (Top right) On July 16, 1958, Marines of the 2nd Battalion, 2nd Marines, form the first truck and Amtrac convoy to enter Beirut. (Bottom left) Marines debark at Beirut International Airport en route to positions on the Lebanon beachhead, July 1958. Just 24 years later another Marine unit would take up positions at the same location. (Bottom right) A Marine reconnaissance patrol moves out at a three-pace interval across the hills of Beirut, July 1958. The 1958 peacekeeping mission ended successfully, particularly when compared to the ill-fated peacekeeping mission of 1982-1984 when 220 Marines were killed after a terrorist truck bomb exploded in their barracks.

(Top) Marines and South Vietnamese Popular Forces of Combined Action Group 4 open fire on a sniper while on patrol south of Quang Tri City on August 28, 1968. The Combined Action Program, in which Marines worked with villagers to resist the Viet Cong, was one of the most successful operations in South Vietnam. (Bottom) U.S. Marines used many special operations techniques in Vietnam in support of the overall war effort. Here, Marines from the 7th Fleet Amphibious Ready Group and an interpreter from the Republic of Vietnam talk with a village elder during Operation Daggerthrust.

(Top left) Effective use of helicopters in combat, first pioneered by Marines in Korea, was perfected in Vietnam. (Top right) This wounded Marine awaits helicopter evacuation to an aid station in the Demilitarized Zone, South Vietnam, on July 31, 1966. (Bottom) A Marine from the 1st Force Reconnaissance Company jumps from an OV-10A Bronco over Red Beach, five miles north of Da Nang, South Vietnam. Recon Marines conducted many special operations in Vietnam.

(Top) The operations officer (S-3) of the 22nd MEU (SOC), at center, meets with one of rebel leader Charles Taylor's representatives on a rainy beach at Port Buchanon, Liberia. A handful of unarmed Marines went ashore to evacuate civilians from the German Embassy in the summer of 1990. *(Photo by LCpl. Don Chouinard Jr.)* (Bottom) A CH-46 from the Air Combat Element of the 22nd MEU (SOC) evacuates civilians from Liberia, 1990. *(Photo by SSgt. John Lavallee)*

(Top right) Engineers from MSSG-22 and the Aviation Combat Element from HMM-261, both of the 22nd MEU (SOC), siphon ocean water off the coast of Liberia for desalinization into drinking water. *(Photo by SSgt. John Lavallee)* (Center left) Sgt. Daniel Z. Vasquez on board a CH-46 en route to the U.S. embassy. The 22nd MEU (SOC) landed 237 Marines in the embassy compound in Monrovia, Liberia, on August 5, 1990. *(Photo by SSgt. John Lavallee)* (Bottom left) During Noncombatant Evacuation Operations in Liberia, Marines from 22nd MEU (SOC) man a machine gun position. *(Photo by JO1 Alan Yuenco)* (Bottom right) Civilians are evacuated from the U.S. embassy in war-stricken Monrovia, Liberia, by CH-46 helicopters in August 1990. *(Photo by JO1 Alan Yuenco)*.

(Top) A lone Marine guards ''Checkpoint 79'' near the Beirut airport in October 1983, just days before more than 240 Marines, Sailors, and Soldiers were killed in their barracks by a terrorist truck bomb. (Bottom) Marines from Hotel Company, BLT 2/4, of the 22d MEU board CH-46 helicopters from HMM-261 to depart from the American Embassy in Monrovia, Liberia, on August 13, 1990. The troops were relieved of their security mission by a reinforced Echo Company. *(Photo by SSgt. John Lavallee)* (Overleaf, page 26) The ability to fly close to urban buildings by day or night in order to insert Marines on rooftops for possible hostage rescue, rapid reinforcement of on-site units, or to assault a terrorist headquarters is an essential skill of USMC units with special-operations capabilities. The UH-1 helicopter from HMM-264 hovers in position while eight Marines fastrope down to the target.

CHAPTER 1 LOW-INTENSITY CONFLICTS

AS THE TWENTIETH CENTURY comes to a close and the risk of another major war in Central Europe seems to have diminished, new hot points challenge the United States. How to deal with them has become a major subject of debate, dollars, and defense planning.

The primary concern today is the low-intensity conflict (LIC), which the U.S. Department of Defense defines as a "political-military confrontation between contending states or groups below conventional war and above the routine, peaceful competition among states. It frequently involves protracted struggles of competing principles and ideologies. Low-intensity conflict ranges from subversion to the use of armed force. It is waged by a combination of means employing political, economic, informational, and military instruments. Low-intensity conflicts are often localized, generally in the Third World, but contain regional and global security implications."

The Pentagon, the White House, and others believe LIC is the most likely form of combat U.S. troops will encounter in the future. LIC may involve small guerilla groups, drug lords, or religious fanatics who challenge the United States. Add the ever-present threat of terrorism, which some believe is an LIC in its own right, and one finds situations calling for just the right mixture of skills and tools to combat terrorists, fight insurgents, and escort civilians to safety.

The term "low-intensity conflict" may be new, but engaging in LIC has long been the bread and butter of the Marine Corps. Its history is rich in expeditionary operations, including two unforgettable events that occurred early in the history of the Corps: the amphibious raid on Britain's Nassau Island in 1776 to deprive the British of much needed ammunition supplies and the famous exploits of USMC Lieutenant Presley O'Bannon and his seven Marines, who in 1805 helped eliminate the threat of Barbary pirates in Libya. The former was, in concept, very similar to the quick, rapid-strike raids Marine Expeditionary Units train for today. The latter gave the Corps the curved Mameluke officer's sword and part of a line for the Marines' Hymn: ". . . to the shores of Tripoli."

"The Marine Corps can land on foreign territory without it being considered an act of war," Secretary of War Patrick J. Hurley wrote in 1931, "but when the Army moves on foreign territory, that is an act of war. That is one of the reasons for the Marine Corps."

Prior to World War II, the Corps was called into action some 139 times, mostly in small skirmishes and conflicts. Since 1945, the majority of operations involving marine and naval forces have been undertaken in order to prevent war, limit its escalation, or protect American civilians and interests.

According to USMC Major Thomas C. Linn, "The Marine Corps came to be regarded on the domestic and international scene as a limited and temporary means by which the United States could exert and resolve conflict without the Nation being committed to war."

The Marine Corps sees an important distinction between LIC and special operations. The former "small war" is fought with conventional means and tactics and is not defined by how much time it takes. Special operations, however, are typically of limited duration and may be employed in large-scale wars, LIC, or during peacetime. The failed rescue mission in 1980 in Iran was a special operation. The U.S. invasion of Panama in December 1989 was a combination of both: an LIC preceded and supported by extensive special operations.

The unsuccessful April 1980 mission in Iran underscored the inadequacy of U.S. special-operations forces, and the Pentagon began developing ways to overcome the problems encountered at "Desert One." At that time the various special-operations forces were short on specialized equipment, such as sophisticated night-vision systems. They lacked the opportunity to train together to develop vital unit cohesiveness and, more importantly, a clear definition of their mission.

In 1984 the Joint Chiefs of Staff sought to resolve the ambiguity. They defined special operations as "operations conducted by specially trained, equipped, and organized Department of Defense forces against strategic or tactical targets in pursuit of national military, political, economic, or psychological objectives. These operations may be conducted during periods of peace or hostilities. They may support conventional operations, or they may be prosecuted independently when the use of conventional forces is either inappropriate or infeasible."

The four U.S. military services, each in its own way, have since built up or expanded their special-operations capabilities, which vary widely in scope and manpower employed. Operating as the Army Special Operations Command (ARSOC), the Army has gathered under one roof the Rangers, Army Special Forces, Delta Force, a Psychological Operations Group (PsyOps), a Signals and Intelligence Group, and the 160th Aviation Regiment. The U.S. Navy has its own Special Warfare Command, known as NAVSPEC-WARCOM, which includes elements of its famed SEALs and special boat squadrons. The Air Force has formed the 23rd AF with a wide range of highly specialized aircraft.

For the Marines the move toward developing special-operations capabilities came only after some soul searching. "A number of senior Marines, including now-retired Marine Commandant General P.X. Kelley," recalled Brigadier General James M. Myatt, "maintained that the Marine Corps was all 'special operations' anyway—a stance easily understandable considering the Corps' history—and no real change was required."

When the Pentagon started to formulate a new policy for special operations following the debacle at Desert One, some attempts were made to have the Marine Corps designated as the single special-operations force in the United States. Those efforts failed, and as a result, all services have developed or enhanced special-operations capabilities.

Of three options determined to be available to the Marine Corps in 1983—to do nothing, to bring back the World War II Raiders, or to enhance existing forces—the third option was picked. Doing nothing and maintaining that the Corps could handle every possible task was considered unrealistic in view of the increasing pressure from Congress on the armed forces to develop special-operations skills. Reviving the Raiders was unacceptable for the same reason that caused their ultimate dissolution after World War II: an elite force such as the Marine Corps does not easily accept another elite force within it.

"Historically that has not worked for us," said Major General Myatt, the first commander of a Marine Corps special-operations-capable unit, the 26th Marine Amphibious Unit, in 1985.

The third option, to "enhance the capabilities of our forward deployed units," General Myatt said, was selected and resulted in what are now known as Marine Expeditionary Units (Special-Operations Capable), or MEU (SOC).

In 1984 Headquarters Marine Corps directed its major East Coast command, Fleet Marine Force Atlantic (FMFLANT) in Norfolk, Virginia, to examine the SOC concept and then start up a pilot program. The present Commandant, General A.M. Gray, then a Lieutenant General and the Commanding General of FMFLANT, was instrumental in getting SOC operations off the ground. Personally, he helped to write the definitions of the basic special-operations missions.

''The more you sweat in peace, the less you bleed in war,'' is an oft-heard saying in the Corps. A Marine's training never stops. Whether running obstacle courses or learning how to place accurate fire during an ambush, Marines learn the value of team work and preparation for the stress of battle.

The Corps insisted that such operations be amphibious in nature and not needlessly duplicate special-operations forces or capabilities already available in other services. The end result was that today's Marine Expeditionary Unit must be able to execute 18 different types of missions, ranging from amphibious raids to the evacuation of civilians.

When the Corps started the current program, it drew not only upon its own history, but it also looked at successful special-operations forces in other nations. Traces of the famous Royal Marine Commandos, the BBE of the Royal Dutch Marines, the GSG-9 unit of the West German Border Patrol, Britain's Special Air Service (SAS), and other special-operations forces were woven into the fabric of the new program.

What the Corps is striving for, General Myatt said, "is a new commitment to excellence." But excellence requires hard work and, in the case of the military where rapid change is virtually unheard of (and some would say impossible to achieve in peacetime), a willingness to persevere. Despite the obstacles, the Marines initiated the new program in June 1985, and the first MEU (SOC) left the United States for the Mediterranean in December 1985.

Six Marine Expeditionary Units rotate on routine deployments to the Mediterranean and the Pacific Rim. Only the two forward-deployed MEUs, one in each theater, are formally designated as "Special-Operations Capable." Earning the SOC designation requires the completion of a rigorous, six-month predeployment training program in which regular line units are trained and equipped to perform special-operations tasks along with more conventional duties. This extensive training is followed by a "final exam" that Lieutenant Colonel Matthew E. Broderick has described as a "Super Bowl of an exercise." It is designed to test the unit on its newly acquired capabilities. Once accomplished, the unit, now ready to deploy, earns the coveted SOC label, which it keeps until the end of its deployment, when another training cycle commences.

"One benefit of having every unit earn that designation over and over is that lessons learned from the last cycle can be incorporated, making the whole thing a form of institutionalized learning," said Colonel Dave Nobel, the officer in charge of the Special Operations Training Group in Camp Lejeune, North Carolina. "Every MEU that goes out is typically just a bit better than the previous unit."

The cyclic training stands as one of the principal differences between the Marine Corps' approach to special operations and what other services do. Army, Navy, and Air Force have each formed specialized groups that train only for special operations. In the Corps the special-operations capability is one of many skills Marines acquire as an expansion of basic skills.

This is not to say that the Marine Corps has only a moderate commitment to developing special-operations capabilities. Quite the contrary. Due to the nature of the Corps, any unit that deploys must be able to conduct a variety of missions, some of which may fall under the classification of "special operations."

(Top and facing) Small rubber boats are perfect for clandestine raids because they present virtually no radar profile and make little noise. (Bottom) Marines land on a beach in Turkey. Behind them rise the hills of Gallipoli, the site of a British-Australian amphibious landing in 1915 that failed miserably. It proved instructive to U.S. Marines, however, who continued to believe that amphibious raids could be successful if properly executed.

Grabbing onto a rope dangling from a helicopter and sliding with your hands and feet to the ground 80 feet below—all while carrying weapons and a full pack—may appear difficult, but in reality, "fastroping," as the technique is called, is rather easy to learn. With this essential skill, Marines can reinforce ships on high seas that have no helicopter landing platforms.

Think of the hijacking of TWA Flight 847 in 1984, the act of piracy on the cruise liner *Achille Lauro* in 1984, and the hostages being held in captivity in Lebanon since 1985. While many stress that hostage rescue may be the least likely mission, if up against a tight deadline and assuming that no time is available to bring in specialized forces from other U.S. services, Marines deployed in the Mediterranean could be the only option.

The U.S. Marines and U.S. Navy, independent from land bases and problems such as overflight rights, only have to deal with nautical distance. Within the Med, most shores are just two or three sailing days or helicopter flying hours away, depending on where the fleet happens to be at the time. The Army's Delta Force would first have to deploy from the United States and then find some kind of base in the region from which to operate. Forward-deployed special-operations-capable units, on the other hand, are often in the vicinity of terrorist incidents, especially those that occur along the Mediterranean littoral. These units must possess the skills to either support the special forces of other services or respond directly in life-threatening, or "in-extremis," instances. Action will be taken in an in-extremis situation when loss of life is imminent, such as when negotiations have broken down and terrorists have started to execute hostages, or when any other action but intervention would lead to further deaths.

In August 1990, along with other armed forces, the United States deployed the First Marine Expeditionary Force to Saudi Arabia. Incorporated into this unit of about 50,000 Marines were several units that had earned or were in the process of earning the SOC designation. The situation in the Persian Gulf called for both conventional military skills and that basket of special-operations capabilities perfected by smaller units.

(Top) In southern Sardinia, Italy, a crew chief of a UH-1 Huey helicopter provides close-in fire support with a mounted M60 machine gun. (Bottom) Rigid Raiding Crafts are new in the Corps' inventory. These modified Boston Whalers have firm bottoms for more stability and can be launched from any of the ships of an amphibious task force.

CHAPTER 2 THE MEU (SOC)

COLONEL JOHN B. CREEL JR. stands six feet three inches tall. When you see him in his stateroom peering intently at his computer through eye glasses that reflect a greenish light, he looks more like a scientist or a professor than a Marine officer.

As an artilleryman, numbers and calculations are second nature to him. Many factors have to be taken into account to place a round precisely on the enemy, and he was trained in the days when wind speed, humidity, air temperature, temperature of the powder, distance to the target, and more were calculated by hand or slide rule. He mastered his trade in the crucible of Vietnam, as his two Silver Stars, two Bronze Stars, and Purple Heart attest.

Colonel Creel commanded the 26th MEU from 1987 to 1990 and took that SOC-qualified unit on two deployments to the Mediterranean. Perfection is high on his list of priorities, as is hard, realistic training. "That," he and other experienced commanders will say repeatedly, "saves lives in the real thing."

(Above) Colonel John B. "Bulldog" Creel, Jr., for two years the stern and effective commander of the 26th Marine Expeditionary Unit. (Facing) Four CH-53E Super Stallions, such as the one seen here, are assigned to the MEU's composite aviation squadron. This powerful, versatile helicopter can lift almost any aircraft or vehicle used by the Marine Corps.

Colonel Creel's personal call sign is "Bulldog," and I often heard him on the radio during operations issuing terse instructions. The name fits him, and it fits his MEU, which is a surprisingly powerful unit for being the smallest of several deployable Marine Corps units that combine ground forces with air support.[1] The Marine Corps is unique in integrating air, ground, and support forces under one command.

Colonel Creel commanded four major groups in the MEU: a reinforced helicopter squadron, a reinforced infantry battalion, an MEU Service Support Group, and a command element that, in addition to running the whole show, contained a host of specialists ranging from experts at reconnaissance and clandestine actions to counterintelligence. Altogether about 2,300 Marines and some 100 Sailors and Navy officers made up the 26th MEU.

"This is probably the most exciting command I have ever had," Colonel Creel said. "You get to deal with all aspects of the Marine Corps and with the Navy."

For Colonel Creel and other MEU commanders, controlling the various organizations and making them work together as a team was a major challenge. He provided steady leadership, often by example. When the 26th MEU tested a new rig for fastroping from CH-53 helicopters—a scary affair causing sweaty palms even for the experienced—he was one of the first down the rope.

The center of all activity, where all the instructions and orders come from, is the MEU's command element, some 130 men strong. Because of the Corps' emphasis on developing special-operations capabilities, the command element has been enhanced with a variety of specialists, such as the Force Reconnaissance Company Detachment, which can be inserted by surface, subsurface (by submarine or with scuba diving gear), or parachute for deep reconnaissance. The Recon Detachment also conducts "direct action," a term

(Top) To assist commanders in planning effective assaults in only six hours, Marines from the Terrain Analysis Support Team build scale models of proposed raid sites. (Bottom) A Marine from the MEU's Air Naval Gun Fire Liaison Company practices with a signal mirror.

encompassing delicate jobs like clandestine raids and hostage recovery.

The Radio Battalion Detachment offers know-how in electronic warfare and signals intelligence. These specialists in encryption can break other people's radio codes, jam enemy radios or overcome the jamming of their own radios, and determine the location of an enemy radio position in order to call in fire. They can listen in on enemy radio conversation and, supported by the MEU's translators, provide the commander with timely intelligence.

The Detachment from the Marine Air Control Group provides the MEU with the ability to extend the air command and control capabilities of the Amphibious Task Force ashore, ensuring coordination between aircraft employment and other supporting arms.

Intelligence is critical; therefore, intelligence specialists "should be part of the MEU, live with them, and know their intentions," said one young intelligence officer. Today's strong intelligence support partially results from the problems the Marines encountered in Beirut from 1982 to 1984. "After the bombing, it was determined that one of the major shortcomings was lack of intelligence support on the scene," one Marine officer said.

"We continuously analyze data to figure out where the next trouble spot could be," explained another officer. "Just imagine there is trouble, major riots, in a country at the Med that could lead to a threat for American civilians and the embassy there. We would start picking up that information and if warranted start collecting other data to be able to execute an NEO [Noncombatant Evacuation Operation]. That doesn't mean we will do it or anybody has told us to do so, but we have to be prepared."

Typical of how suddenly situations can evolve was the insurrection in Liberia. In the summer of 1990, the United States and many other nations were caught unawares by the escalating civil war in that country, and the MEU (SOC) on station in the Med was ordered off the coast of Monrovia to prepare for an NEO. The five Navy ships carrying the MEU were positioned just beyond the horizon from Liberia for months waiting for word on how to respond.

Support for the intelligence operation comes from the Fleet Imagery Interpretation Unit Detachment and the Terrain Analysis Support Team. These experts analyze often hazy, black-and-white photographs to figure out key terrain features and other information. The pictures come from a variety of sources, including reconnaissance flights of the MEU's Harrier jump jets and helicopters, satellite pictures, or existing intelligence files. "They would work with pictures of the embassy complex and a nearby landing zone or beach to generate information on how many helicopters could land in that zone," explained one officer. "That is important in determining how quickly we can conduct an evacuation."

Often, and as time permits, these Marines will build terrain models, which may be small and hastily put together or elaborate constructions. Using Lego® building blocks, paper, sand, polyurethane foam, and other tools familiar to any modeler, they can create scale models of almost anything. Such models allow raid-force commanders to study the ground and come up with options. In 35 days spent on ship off the coast of Beirut in 1989, a terrain model of one particular facility evolved into a masterpiece, complete with trees, bushes, sand, and other details.

Each MEU travels with a detachment of the Air Naval Gunfire Liaison Company (ANGLICO). Its primary mission is to support U.S. allies or U.S. Army troops by calling in air or naval gunfire. U.S. Marine Corps units have their own experts, normally assigning artillery officers to call in naval gunfire and pilots to direct air support. During NATO exercises in the Med, ANGLICO traveled and lived with Italian Marine and Army units, Turkish Marines, Portuguese naval infantry, and Spanish Marines.

Other support includes interrogators and translators, counterintelligence experts, and an air defense detachment.[2]

"This is an impressive group," says Colonel Creel. "We have many of the capabilities you would find in other armed forces only on a division level or maybe on a brigade level." As he points out, an MEU must operate far from home and be able to make immediate use of such support without waiting for it to arrive. The underlying premise of the MEU (SOC) concept is that time to plan is likely to be limited. Among the many factors that turn a regular line unit into a special-operations-capable unit is the ability to plan and execute a mission in just six hours.

"To be able to react within six hours," stressed Colonel Creel, "gives you the advantage of speed and surprise," essential ingredients for victory. Being held

(Below) Marines deploy on a beach in Turkey. (Facing) CH-53E Super Stallions on maneuvers.

to a six-hour planning cycle forces a unit to prepare for all possible contingencies and gives the U.S. President a tremendous weapon, a "quick reaction strike force," the colonel said. The enemy is unlikely to expect such a swift response.

While an MEU can operate for about 15 days or longer ashore with its own resources, it is also the "forward element of something much bigger," Marine Commandant General A.M. Gray said. In case of major hostilities, an MEU could prepare the ground for a larger unit such as a Marine Expeditionary Brigade. It could secure an area as a base for follow-on forces. For most of this century, seizing advanced naval bases has been one of the primary missions of the Corps.

The Commandant's words were put to the test in 1990 when Marines deployed to Saudi Arabia. First, Marines drawn from units aboard ship and close by occupied an area near the Persian Gulf and just south of the Kuwait-Saudi Arabian border. Follow-on forces in the form of three Marine Expeditionary Brigades—organized as one Marine Expeditionary Force—then moved into the area held by the smaller unit. Among the many units deployed to the Gulf was the Second Battalion, Eighth Marines, which is featured later in this book.

The whole MEU travels on three to five Navy amphibious ships and draws on extensive naval support, such as medical resources, gunfire, and stable platforms for the helicopter squadron. Amphibious warfare ships come in a wide range of types and sizes. One of the most common types—the LPH (Landing Platform, Helicopter)—allows helicopters to land on its flight deck and can be used for helo-borne attacks. The LSD (Landing Ship, Dock), another common ship, can be used to launch Amtracs or small raiding craft from its well deck for surface assaults. The LHA and the LHD (Amphibious Assault Ship, Multi-Purpose), typified

by the new USS *Wasp*, combine both functions, offering a well deck and a flight deck.

While they lack the grace of a frigate, amphibious ships, often large, ugly, gray hulks, exist for just one purpose: to move Marines across the beach against a determined foe.

During the predeployment phase, an MEU trains with the naval forces with which it will ultimately deploy. Thus, MEU (SOC) development entails integration into the surface Navy structure, building an inter-service team capable of meeting challenges quickly.

In the Med an MEU is assigned to the Sixth Fleet; in the Pacific, the Seventh Fleet. In addition to having his "own" Marines, the Navy fleet commander often commands some 30 ships, which are built around a carrier battle group, and a surface action battle group, which is built around a battleship like the USS *Iowa* or USS *New Jersey*. The fleet is highly mobile and versatile.

The term "Blue/Green Team" or "Navy/Marine Corps Team" has been around for a long time. The "Blue" side contributes the Sea Air Land (SEAL) Teams, which work with the MEU and are integrated into the MEU for most special operations. While the SEALs are the Navy's own "special-operations force," they fulfill more than just that one role. Their traditional missions still include activities such as underwater demolition and reconnoitering a beach prior to an assault.

The MEU, the "Green" side, provides the fighters, the power projection landing force. It is known as the Landing Force Sixth Fleet (LF6F) in the Med.

As recently as 10 years ago, there were frequent conflicts between the two naval services. Today, while the relationship is complex, the MEU commander and his Navy counterpart, the commodore commanding the amphibious squadron, work hand in hand on all issues.

The MEU operates in the Mediterranean Sea as part of the Navy's Sixth Fleet. The ships that constituted a key element of that fleet in the summer of 1989 are (left to right, back row to front row) the FF-1090 *Ainsworth*, CGN-38 *Virginia*, *LPD-12 *Shreveport*, *LST-1197 *Barnstable County*, FF-1081 *Aylwin*, CG-56 *Jacinto*, AD-44 *Shenandoah*, CV-43 *Coral Sea*, *LHA-4 *Nassau*, FFG-42 *Klakring*, AE-27 *Butte*, AO-178 *Monongahela*, FFG-59 *Kauffman*, SSN-694 *Groton*, DDG-3 *John King*. Those marked by an asterisk were used by the deployed MEU (SOC).

Within the amphibious forces, a true team spirit exists. In the Med the Navy counterpart to the MEU is the amphibious squadron, which is called the Mediterranean Amphibious Ready Group (MARG). It provides the ships, which serve as strategic transportation, accommodations, launch platforms, warehouses, and restaurants for the MEU.

During the six-month deployment, the USS *Nassau*, LHA-4, became home to some 2,000 Marines, who developed many colorful nicknames for the ship, including "Luxury Hotel Afloat" (a play on the LHA acronym), "Homebase Alpha," and "The Death Star." Once I overheard an airborne CH-53E pilot ask his copilot, "You want to go back to 'Mother'?"

Ships are often compared to small cities, the USS *Nassau*, more often than others. Post office, store, sewage plant, and barber shop are each contained within her hulls. A major amphibious ship of the type typically deployed to the Mediterranean, the *Nassau* also has a 300-bed hospital and four operating rooms.

On one of the Navy's super-carriers, the population can exceed 5,000 people. Amphibious ships, such as the USS *Nassau*, a floating island 20 stories tall and some 850 feet long, boast a population of 4,000. For many Marines and Sailors, these are often the largest "cities" they have ever lived in, and like any city or town, the ships are worlds where newcomers are greeted with a delightful mixture of suspicion and hearty welcome.

Marines settle in quickly aboard ship. It is part of their training, tradition, and trade. Without Marines to transport and support, ships such as the USS *Nassau* would be virtual ghosts.

Aboard ship, space is at a premium, so being able to live at close quarters with others is an absolute

After spending six months in the LHA-4 USS *Nassau*, nicknamed "Luxury Hotel Afloat," Marines know why "cruise" is not the right term for a deployment. Aboard ship space is at a premium, so bunks are stacked three to five high. When the air conditioning fails, the heat becomes unbearable.

necessity. Only a few, such as the ship's captain, the commodore, and the colonel commanding all Marines, have quarters that compare favorably to more spacious land-based facilities. For the rest, especially the troops, space is severely limited, with 25 men living together in an area the size of a typical hotel room, sleeping in bunks stacked three to five high. Ships are built air tight, partially as a defense against chemical warfare. When the air conditioning fails in 90-plus degree weather, the smells of men and machinery overpower you before the heat and humidity ever get a chance.

Space seems to shrink even more during those times when there is little to do. Training exercises and physical workouts help keep troops occupied, but when the weather turns bad or flight operations are in full swing, time on the flight deck is restricted. It is a credit to the Marines' discipline (reinforced by a stiff $400 fine) that fist fights are few.

During almost six months aboard the USS *Nassau*, I learned to accept the discomforts of ship life as routine, even though only six feet above my head in my narrow Navy bunk was the flight deck, separated from me by a mere 10 inches of metal. Since the Harriers took off right above where I slept, everything shook when they went to full power. I quickly learned to tape down my alarm clock and to secure all loose gear, because the enormous vibrations of the Harriers caused them to fall off their tables or ledges and onto the floor.

Another "challenge" I learned to live with was the constant presence of the metallic voice on the public address system, which is known as a 1MC on ship. Announcements are made constantly; in fact, about four times a day the 1MC broadcast, "This is a test...one...two...three. Test complete." I never learned the purpose of the frequent tests, but I quickly became adept at screening out all but the messages that mattered.

(Top) Landing an aircraft on the flight deck of the USS *Nassau* at night or in rough weather demands constant practice and total concentration by even the most experienced pilots. (Bottom) Marine Major Steve ''Buckwheat'' Patton, HMM-264 Harrier pilot, poses with his airplane.

CHAPTER 3 SPECIAL PURPOSE FORCE

"IF YOU WANT TO play in special operations you better become a night owl," a major once told me.

To a special-operations-capable Marine, the less moon the better. Waiting for just the right moment is a critical ingredient for special operations, but at night when all the sounds of the day have gone away, waiting is harder. Night-vision goggles, which enable their wearers to "see in the dark," become bulkier as the night drags on. You move only a little. You have to be silent.

The target this night was a small wooden building, a simulated terrorist headquarters at the edge of the woods. Eight terrorists, or "Tangos" in radio language, reportedly held four Americans hostage.

A team consisting mostly of Marines from 2nd Force Reconnaissance Company attached to the 26th MEU intended to rescue them, destroy the headquarters, capture the terrorists for "prosecution in the United States," and pick up everything of intelligence value. They planned to come in over the water in Rigid Raiders and leave by helicopter. Standard operating procedure in special operations, explained MEU Commander Colonel Creel, dictates that "you come in one way, and leave by another" to avoid being ambushed by the enemy.

Wearing night-vision goggles, I started making out the first shapes. The team of 12 men emerged from the woods. They had come in hours earlier, stowing their small, fast boats deep in a nearby inlet. The hidden vessels would serve as a second extraction route in case of problems with the helicopters. The team had remained hidden in the woods until the appointed hour for their silent, slow approach to the target.

There was complete silence. Radio communications were reserved for calling in the helicopters or for serious emergencies.

The team, visible only through the goggles, moved up to the porch of the small building. They "stacked up" next to the two doors, clustered in a small group, and attached explosive charges to the doors to create an "explosive breach." Within seconds a quick explosion resounded, followed almost immediately by a muffled cry inside the building. One Marine broke a window, fired a smoke grenade into the building. Then they were in.

"Hours before this assault, we had worked out and rehearsed who was going to do what," one Marine explained. "We had a floor plan, partially wrong as it turned out, but that was the best intelligence we had. We made a small mockup and decided who was going to take out what corner, who was going to secure the hostages, who was going to collect intelligence. Everybody had a specific job, and we trained for it."

The Marines have evolved certain techniques for action inside buildings, but the specifics are trade secrets. "You don't want terrorists to know what you are going to do," Captain Steve Zotti, officer in charge of the Recon Marines, said.

Less than a minute or two passed. Weapons were fired. Then, the Marines emerged with the hostages and a tied-up terrorist. They rushed to a nearby field.

One Marine activated a firefly—a small infrared strobe the size of a Zippo® lighter and only visible with night-vision goggles. It marked the helicopter landing zone, and within a few minutes, the first of two CH-46 helicopters descended, just clearing a web of high-tension wires. The freed hostages and captured terrorist, under guard, boarded the first helo, while the rest of the team followed on the second.

From the moment the first shapes emerged soundlessly from the tree line to the instant that the last helicopter departed, only six minutes had elapsed.

At a compound in Camp Lejeune, North Carolina, called Stone Bay, Marines train to enter buildings, fire weapons, and incapacitate terrorists without harming hostages. A "shooting gallery" consisting of a building

Almost all special operations occur at night in order to take advantage of the cover of darkness and the enemy's fatigue. Here a hostage rescue mission is recorded by a camera fitted with a night-vision lens.

(Top) Marines prepare to "rush" a building during hostage rescue training. They wear "black gear"—flame-resistant flight suits and vests—and carry MP-5 submachine guns. (Bottom) Occasionally "aggressors" and "assault troops" train hand-to-hand.

with full-sized rooms furnished with castoff couches, chairs, and desks is used to simulate a variety of hostage situations. The walls are covered with a heavy, rubber-like substance capable of capturing live rounds and keeping them from penetrating the outside walls. Dummies of terrorists and hostages are placed in various positions throughout.

Before any "attack" on the facility, the Marines work up a plan on who will do what, using the best available intelligence on the suspected number of terrorists and hostages present. "That information is normally wrong, and that's on purpose," said one Marine. "You have to learn to adjust quickly."

Marines then rush the building, break down the doors, quickly identify who is who, and incapacitate the bad guys. "It takes some practice," a staff sergeant with the unit dryly commented.

In most training scenarios the rooms are dark to simulate the loss of electricity or diminished visibility from smoke grenades. The only illumination is provided by a strong flash light taped to the barrel of an MP-5, a German-made submachine gun,

long a favorite of anti-terrorist forces and African palace guards.

The scenarios prepared for at the compound come as close to the real thing as they possibly can short of using actual people. "It forces you to make split-second decisions," a young corporal with the unit commented. "You cannot hesitate. You have no room to move, no time. And if you screw up, the guy you are rescuing is dead. No second chances." Skills learned in rescuing hostages can be applied to a variety of other missions, such as the United States' 1990 efforts to capture Manuel Noriega in Panama.

The 50 or so people who are specifically trained for these missions are organized as the strike unit of the Maritime Special Purpose Force (MSPF). Typically composed of Force Reconnaissance and other specially trained Marines and supported by Navy SEALs, they are, in official Marine Corps language, "an evolutionary organization of Navy & Marine units designed to optimize forces available to conduct highly sensitive and complex special missions." Their expertise includes small-boat operations, scuba

The MP-5 submachine gun fires 9 mm rounds at up to 350 rounds per minute and is used exclusively by the MEU's Force Reconnaissance Detachment. This one is equipped with a flashlight to allow its user to direct fire in the dark.

diving, demolition techniques, cliff climbing and assault, navigating sewer systems, and close-quarter battles inside buildings.

Skilled in "deep reconnaissance," MSPF members are able to operate unseen far behind enemy lines and collect timely intelligence. They possess a wide range of techniques for inserting into a hostile environment. With the aid of large altimeters on their wrists and oxygen masks on their faces, they can parachute from 30,000-foot heights without opening their chutes until 3,000 to 1,000 feet above the ground. This technique, known as a HALO (High Altitude-Low Opening) jump, offers a clandestine means by which to enter an area.

In addition the MSPF can jump with specially rigged chutes that enables it to navigate and arrive with almost pinpoint accuracy. "You could move some 20 miles from where you get dropped off by the plane," said one jumper.

SEALs in support of the MSPF can be dropped off on enemy shores by submarines. Two, the USS *Sam Houston* and USS *John Marshall*, were converted for special-operations use in years past.

Navy SEALs also conduct beach surveys to prepare amphibious landings. This includes mapping out the beach gradient, determining where there are underwater obstacles—big rocks or deep holes, for example—and understanding the effects of tide and currents.

As with all missions conducted by an MEU, the MSPF relies on the support of helicopters from the air combat element and infantry detachments from the battalion.

The list of tasks for which the MSPF is qualified is impressive. These include nighttime clandestine raids that could involve taking out a radar tower near an airfield preparatory to a bigger force from the MEU seizing the airfield. An American consulate under

During a high-altitude, low-opening (HALO) jump, an aircraft flies close to the drop zone at approximately 30,000 feet. Once the parachutists exit the aircraft, they remain invisible by delaying the opening of their chutes until 3,000 to 1,000 feet above the ground. Oversized altimeters worn on their wrists enable them to know when to open the parachutes.

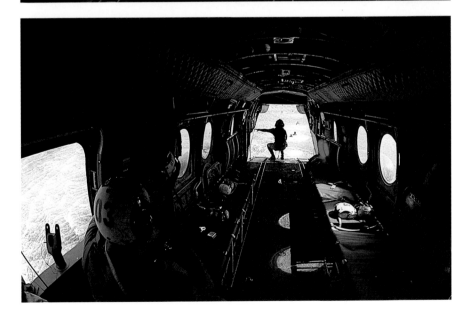

(Top, center, and bottom left) CH-46 Sea Knight helicopters frequently ferry Marines into "hot" landing zones or drop them by parachute. (Top right) While all Force Reconnaisance Marines are parachute qualified, only some are qualified to jump into the sea. Once in the water, they swim to rubber boats that have also been dropped by aircraft and use them to return to shore.

(Top left) The rectangular chute can be used to direct descent more accurately than conventional round parachutes. (Top right) During this amphibious assault, Marines run through the surf toward the beach after being ''driven'' to the shore by Rigid Raiders. (Bottom) A Marine mans a rifle on a Rigid Raider.

A CH-46 helicopter uses a spie rig to extract Marines from difficult terrain.

sudden siege could be reinforced with MSPF members who are skilled in fastroping onto the tops of buildings.

"Our mission is to conduct raids; reinforce U.S. installations such as embassies, consulates, or trade missions; contain incidents involving U.S. interests; recover and extract people or equipment and documents; and, of course, conduct hostage rescue missions in an in-extremis situation," Captain Steve Zotti, the officer in charge of the Marine segment of the MSPF, explained.

I got a sense of how extensive the list of possible missions for this force was during several weeks of training in New Orleans, Louisiana. There, in coordination with the FBI, the MSPF participated in TRUE (Training in an Urban Environment), which takes place several times a year—mostly at night—in major cities throughout the United States. The FBI, which works hand in hand with the Corps on TRUE exercises, selects the cities, critiques many of the missions, and gives practical instruction on techniques to use in clearing rooms and buildings.

"Built-up areas are the most likely battleground," said Captain Zotti. "That's what we have to train for."

Being able to infiltrate an urban area, move about without attracting attention, and collect intelligence are vital to the success of an urban mission. The force has to gain experience in running radio communications in built-up areas, which "presents some major challenges," the communications officer of the MEU said.

In a training city the MSPF and parts of the MEU command element set up missions that involve such things as learning how to take out a power plant.

"Do you have any idea how many switches there are in a control room?" asked one Marine staff sergeant. "You have to learn which one is which, which one to turn to shut it all off, and where to place explosives to turn the whole thing into such a mess that nobody can bring it back up for a while."

The force might also be charged with searching and clearing large buildings. Old, dark, multi-storied warehouses—those with no windows and uncertain floors—are a favorite.

Other types of training scenarios include hostage rescues, which may play out over several days. "Umpires" provide initial intelligence, and then the Marines watch a house or monitor a neighborhood until the hostage recovery is completed.

As a subset of TRUE, Marines also train to disable and blow up oil rigs. "It takes a lot of skill to know what to blow up and how," said a representative of the oil company whose rigs are used for training. "What do you do to shut it all down in the shortest possible time without creating a major oil spill?"

Pilots of the squadron practice landing on rigs, and the Marines become familiar with various rig designs. Such skills came in handy in April 1988 when, in an attempt to keep shipping lanes open in the Persian Gulf and remove installations that were actively interrupting and threatening commercial vessels, the Marine Corps demolished several Iranian oil rigs.

MSPF members appear somewhat different than other Marines and Sailors. They wear their hair longer to avoid being quickly identified as military personnel. They conduct most of their work in "sterile" (unmarked) flight suits, which are made of flame-retardant material and give a measure of protection that other uniforms don't provide. They carry their equipment in large black vests known as "black gear." The vests hold ammunition magazines and pouches containing a variety of tools, all fastened by Velcro, which facilitates rearranging the pouches to meet individual requirements. Typically, MSPF members carry two weapons, an MP-5 9mm submachine gun and, depending on whether the member is a Marine or Navy SEAL, a .45-caliber automatic or a 9mm automatic pistol, respectively. Dressed in their flight suits, covered by black gear, and often wearing black hoods, MSPF members look truly menacing.

One day I went out to watch the Marines from the Second Force Reconnaissance Company train. In the hot Spanish sun, they were firing their submachine guns and .45s. They are about the last unit in the Corps to use the .45, which has been extensively modified to include an improved trigger and, in most cases, a flashlight mounted to the barrel for close-in fighting in buildings.

The men were being taught the art of shooting by instinct, a skill that involves aiming a weapon with the body rather than with an eye on the sight. The technique is used in night combat or for fighting in confined spaces.

"You don't have time to carefully aim," their lieutenant said. "You will be at close quarters, and you have to be able to shoot fast. Shooting by instinct . . . that's what counts."

"Instinctive firing" was first taught during World War II by British Major William E. Fairbairn to the young British Special Operations Executive, which had been set up in 1940 to train for operating in Axis territory. In addition to advocating this skill, Major Fairbairn, together with a partner, gained lasting fame as the co-developer of the Fairbairn-Sykes commando dagger.

The MSPF uses a variety of specialized tools, such as night-vision goggles and light-intensification devices that permit wearers to see shapes of people and objects in dark rooms. They also use stun grenades ("flash-bangs") developed by Britain's Special Air Squadron. These weapons explode with an ear-splitting bang and give off light of about 50,000 candle power, sufficient to blind anybody in the area. Reportedly, they were used for the first time with great success by Israeli commandos in rescuing hostages held at Entebbe, Uganda, in 1977. During an actual mission flash-bangs would be shot by grenade launchers through a window to stun terrorists for the first critical seconds of an assault. More sophisticated flash-bangs explode like a fire cracker six or seven times in four seconds, increasing the "stun" effect.

"If there is a gadget we don't have yet, we will have it soon," one Marine lieutenant said. "We love gadgets."

(Above) During a ''Soft Duck'' maneuver to insert Reconnaissance Marines, a rubber boat is tossed out of a helicopter, such as this CH-46 Sea Knight, which hovers some 10 to 15 feet above the waves. Marines jump out after the rubber boat and ride it to the beach. (Facing) The .45-caliber automatic pistol seen here has been modified with a flashlight for use in darkened buildings. (Overleaf, pages 54-55) A surprise assault on a building in downtown New Orleans, Louisiana, requires split-second coordination between the assault element, here Marines from the MEU's Maritime Special Purpose Force, and the helicopter pilots. A squad of Marines fastroping from the back of a CH-46 Sea Knight can be inserted in less than 30 seconds.

Landing zones can be evacuated quickly and safely when on-ground teams work closely with the aviation squadron. The air-ground team concept has been a unique feature of the Marine Corps since 1912 when the first Marine aviator reported for duty.

CHAPTER 4 BATTALION LANDING TEAM RAIDS

AN AIRFIELD SEIZURE

MISSION: NLT 2000 (LOCAL) 28 February 1989, G Company will conduct a helicopter-borne raid to seize Camp Davis Airfield from extremists in order to allow the establishment of a noncombatant evacuation site for U.S. personnel in the Country of Carteret. The airfield will be held until relief by Carteret forces or until completion of the Noncombatant Evacuation Operation.

The planning for the airfield raid started the minute the "mission order" was issued to "Golf" Company of the Second Battalion, Eighth Marines.

First, the intelligence officer gave a briefing on the hostile forces suspected at the airfield, on general terrain conditions, and on other factors that could affect the raid planning. The information showed that the airfield was lightly defended by a handful of troops in the vicinity of the "air tower."

In developing the probable scenario, intelligence officer Captain Buddy Rizzio withheld just enough information from the trainees to allow for surprises. The "misinformation" was intended to give trainees a chance to make mistakes and learn from them without serious consequences. The ability to be flexible and adapt to ever-changing situations is invaluable during combat, they learn through practice.

The company's lieutenants gathered maps of the "objective." Company commander Captain Erik Doyle came up with several options on how the company could go about seizing the airfield. The planners—the lieutenants, their captain, and senior NCOs—considered a multitude of factors, including whether there was a need for fire support (such as that provided by Cobra helicopters); the best way to handle communications; electronic warfare, logistical, and medical support requirements; and the kind of rehearsals that were necessary.

Required to develop several courses of action, Captain Doyle and his planners were forced to analyze the objective more thoroughly, determining in the process if there was another, perhaps better way to accomplish their goal. The company commander gave a formal briefing to the battalion commander to get his input and ultimate approval of the plan.

After the general plan was approved by the battalion commander, the company commander worked out the actual course of action, a step-by-step description of how the airfield seizure would proceed. He was able to draw upon existing plans that had been written and rehearsed in the past and that could be adapted to suit the task at hand.

For this operation three heavily armed fast attack vehicles (FAVs) would be dropped off at night some distance from the airfield by helicopter. "At night the enemy's defenses are down," Lieutenant Colonel Matthew Broderick said. "His body clock is geared to sleep. But you have got to do it right."

The drop-off point selected was far enough away from the target that the noise of the helicopters and FAVs would be screened out by favorable wind directions and dense woods. Aided by night-vision goggles, the drivers would approach the field as silently as possible just minutes before the troop transport helicopters arrived. The FAVs would suppress any fire from the suspected enemy concentration and return fire from any unknown source while the helicopters with the main assault element landed. With limited armor and only a few on-board machine guns, CH-46 helos are highly vulnerable on the ground.

The jeep-based team would also be responsible for calling in fire support from the Cobra attack helicopters hovering beyond the tree line. Because of their close proximity and speed, the Cobras could hit within 20 seconds.

After the main assault element came in, one designated platoon would attack and secure the tower, while the remaining Marines would spread out around

(Top) Captain Steve Zotti of the MEU's Maritime Special Purpose Force briefs (bottom right) Lieutenant Colonel Tony Corwin, the battalion's executive officer, and other Marines on a special operation. (Bottom left) Accurate maps are essential for successful missions. (Facing) An abandoned building will house Battalion Landing Team 2/8's Combat Operations Center. To be operational the center needs only a map and an assortment of radios.

goggles to see if the helicopters were visible. Timing is essential to the success of a raid.

"They are late," said the colonel.

"No, Sir, they are just on time," responded operations officer Major Dan Schuster, who had been waiting in another vehicle.

Far off in the distance a quick light passed by, then two. Like fireflies, the lights danced in the air, moving up and down, darting forward and then quickly disappearing behind the tree line at the edge of the airfield just to pop up a few seconds later somewhere else.

"Those are Cobras," the colonel said.

"Snakes," the sergeant major responded. "Snakes in the sky."

On an actual raid the attack helicopters would remain unseen, but here at what was once Camp Davis Field during World War II, safety regulations required the use of navigation lights.

The Cobra gunships were flying picket duty for the raid. In constant radio contact with the raiding force, they could be called in to provide instant fire support with rockets and machine guns capable of dropping a curtain of fire at the rate of 650 rounds a minute.

The "aggressors," Marines located nearby in what was being called the air tower, could be heard stamping their feet to ward off the cold.

Suddenly, out of the dark emerged the shapes of three FAVs armed with heavy .50-caliber machine guns or machine gun-like MK-19 grenade launchers. They sped down an auxiliary runway, turned and stopped next to the air tower, and started firing on the aggressors. The members of the assault force were equipped with night-vision goggles, so they aimed their weapons well.

(The infantry is using NVGs with more frequency in night operations. During the U.S. invasion of Panama, virtually all special-operations forces were equipped with them, as were many regular infantry line units.)

Within minutes, six CH-46 helicopters landed, disgorging Marines who fanned out and quickly secured the perimeter. A firefight with the aggressors ensued.

Guided by the telltale flashes of enemy rifles, Marines moved into position to return fire. Using standard small-unit tactics, one group of Marines provided covering fire while another group advanced against the enemy, drawing a tighter and tighter circle around the air tower. Within minutes the force at the tower was encircled; its inhabitants had either been "killed" or had surrendered. The airfield was declared secure. The elaborately planned operation, from the first sighting of the Cobras to the ensuing firefight and surrender, had taken just 11 minutes, the time of an average coffee break.

"Not fast enough," said Colonel Broderick. "Shock. Surprise. Violence. That's what raids should be." Speed and surprise, he passionately explained, cut down on casualties. The enemy must never have enough time to react. The battalion was ordered to train again.

"My job is to win, first of all, but I also have to minimize casualties," the colonel later explained in a reflective moment while on deployment in the Mediterranean. "I have to use all my skills to maximize the effect and minimize the cost. I always have to ask, 'Is it really worth the life of a young Marine?'"

Training his troops hard, at times to exhaustion, he gives them the proficiency they need to survive. His demands test and develop the young lieutenants in charge of their first platoons, the squad leaders, and those who without such training might make a "dumb move and get a lot of people killed."

AN AMPHIBIOUS ASSAULT

"Now Set Condition 1 Alpha" resounded from the Public Address system, shaking the bodies of sleeping Marines and propelling members of the Battalion Landing Team (BLT) into motion. After putting on web gear and shouldering their packs, the men negotiated the narrow ladders down to the well deck. It was a challenge. Six levels down they went, and on each ladder a pack, harness, rifle, or other piece of gear got hooked on some metal object. The going was slow, and the press of Marines behind the hung-up soldier didn't help.

Once on the well deck of the LST, the men moved into position. One Marine's life vest conflicted with his harness. His buddy helped him out. Another helped him. There was barely enough room between the Amtracs for these courtesies. The time was just after 1 a.m. Even though everybody had had only a few hours of sleep and confusion should have ruled, each Marine quickly found the right Amtrac. The success of this procedure highlighted the importance of the months of training and practice that had preceded the moment.

The Marines settled into their confined spots on the AAVs. Diesel fumes filled each compartment as the Amtracs' engines sprang to life. There was less engine noise than that made by a helicopter taking off but still plenty. The sound was deeper, more resonant, like a convoy of 18-wheel trucks climbing a steep hill.

The USS Nassau's stern gate had been lowered, and we awaited the order to start the assault. As soon as it was given, our Amtracs drove into the water. The waves muffled the noise of the engine, but diesel fumes overwhelmed the hot, narrow, 24-man troop compartment.

"Let nobody vomit now," prayed a staff sergeant and veteran of many such trips to the beach. One seasick man normally leads to others, not pleasant under any circumstances, let alone in a tight space lit inadequately by a single red tactical light.

The voyage seemed to last for hours, but in actuality it took only 30 minutes.

Once on the beach, the Amtrac's rear hatch opened and hit wet sand. Marines rushed out, weapons ready, and moved into position around the tracks. Then they were off to seize the assigned objective.

Using Amtracs, the BLT's mechanized company is a highly mobile force. Virtually all gear can be moved from ship to shore swiftly. Once ashore, however, much of the movement is by foot, which is just as slow as it was in the days of the Roman Legions.

(Above) Some 20 combat-equipped Marines can squeeze in an Assault Amphibious Vehicle or Amtrac for the trip from ship to shore. (Facing) Marines on board the USS Nassau deploy by helicopter from the flight deck or by boats, seen here in the ship's well deck.

To launch from the USS *Barnstable County*, an LST (Landing Ship, Tank), Amtracs drive off the ship's rear ramp and drop into the water. Once ashore, the armored vehicles move by traditional tracks.

For three weeks during the MEU's predeployment work-up, Fort A.P. Hill, Virginia, was home to the 1,400-member Battalion Landing Team, Second Battalion, Eighth Marines (BLT 2/8). The BLT 2/8 practiced everything from basic infantry skills to waging company assaults.

"Everything you see, all this, is here to support me," said Colonel Matthew Broderick (aka "Chomper"), who brimmed with infectious enthusiasm and pride as he walked at a rapid pace across the Fort's over-sized parking lot, which was filled with military vehicles of every type. With all its attachments, the battalion is a powerful instrument, and the colonel's pride was understandable.

Due to the importance of its mission and its size, the BLT dominates the MEU. The MEU's command element, air squadron, and service support group all work together and, very often, in direct support of the BLT.

In planning and training for amphibious landings, Colonel Broderick and his executive officer Lieutenant Colonel Tony Corwin (who later succeeded Colonel Broderick as battalion commander) serve more as teachers than commanders. Under their watchful eyes, their staffs were encouraged to plan, move, and make decisions. During raids, Colonel Broderick and Lieutenant Colonel Corwin often stayed in the background observing, only occasionally coming forward to offer guidance. Their job was to train and pass on the knowledge they had gained through combat experience. The transmission of knowledge from one generation to another is essential to any military organization.

A tall man with a "high-and-tight" haircut, Lieutenant Colonel Corwin is the poster-perfect Marine. One of his most recent assignments was as operations officer at the spit-and-polish capital of the Corps, the Marine Barracks in Washington, D.C. From

(Top) Amtracs line up to form assault waves. (Bottom) The view from inside an Amtrac during an assault is limited. As it crosses the water, the vehicle pitches up and down; seasickness is common.

the parade-ground perfection of that assignment, he was moved to the often chaotic world of commanding an infantry battalion.

The 2/8, the MEU's ground combat element, is the nucleus of the Battalion Landing Team. USMC special-operations battalions (four on each coast) are larger than regular infantry battalions because they have four rifle companies rather than the customary three. The rifle companies serve as the BLT's primary tactical units, its muscle.

"Sly" is the code name for the 2/8's "Fox" Company. In the Mediterranean, operating in great isolation onboard an LST, the USS *Barnstable County*, the company is the only heavy-mechanized force in the BLT. Its role is to come ashore in armored Amtracs, assault a beach, and move inland. The Amtracs, which carry 24 combat-equipped Marines, are launched from the rear of the LST. They cross the water at six or seven knots, looking like gigantic sea turtles. Two of them are equipped as command and control vehicles, carrying at least 15 radios.

"Rowdy's Raiders," the "Echo" Company, full of pride and heart, is the battalion's boat company, a major innovation and part of the MEU (SOC) program. The raiding company is equipped with 15 Rigid Raider Crafts and 15 Combat Rubber Raider Crafts. The Rigid Raiders, oversized Boston Whalers, can be launched from the well deck of a ship, floating from beyond the horizon and approaching the beach silently, almost invisibly until they are less than 100 yards offshore. Since they move fast, they cover the remaining "audible" distance in 10 to 15 seconds. They are perfect for clandestine entry into an environment where the use of helicopters is judged impossible due to a hostile air threat.

"Doc" and "Stepchild," the 2/8's "Golf" and "Hotel" Companies, respectively, operate from the USS *Nassau*. During an amphibious landing, these air assault companies would most probably be designated to seize an objective well inland from the beach.

The four rifle companies are reinforced with detachments from the battalion's weapons company, which is responsible for heavy weapons, such as MK-19 grenade launchers, M60 machine guns, TOW and Dragon antitank rockets (which can also be used to take out bunkers and fortified positions), and 81 mm mortars.

Artillery support comes from Battery H, Third Battalion, Tenth Marines. Known as "Lone Ranger," this unit provides the BLT with long-range fire support using four M101A 105 mm howitzers and four M198 155 mm howitzers organized in two platoons. Mobility is provided for the battery by the helicopter squadron, which can lift all equipment and move it far forward.

The MEU can draw on support by naval gunfire; however, such guns—with the exception of the 16-inch guns on the nation's four battleships—can only reach up to 23,000 yards. For targets deeper inland, the BLT's artillery is required. The MEU can also use Harriers and Cobras to provide fire support for troops on the ground.

To defeat enemy tanks, the BLT controls a section of Second Tank Battalion's Anti-Tank Company. This section is equipped with TOW II missiles that can hit targets 3,700 meters away or Dragons that can travel 1,000 meters.

By design, the 26th MEU (SOC)'s light, highly mobile BLT has no tanks, but some armor is provided by a detachment of the 2nd Light Armored Infantry Battalion. The unit is equipped with eight light armored vehicles (LAVs). These eight-wheeled armored vehicles look like miniature tanks mounted on truck chassis, and one of them was decorated with the horn of a rhinoceros, symbolic of the unit's call sign, "Rhino." Missions in which they are used include reconnaissance, screening, and engaging limited objectives. The LAV's high mobility and speed, reported to be in excess of 80 miles per hour, makes it ideal for raids and for missions calling for surprise. Using LAVs, members of the BLT are somewhat akin to the swift, lightly armored hussars of the fifteenth century, who traveled on fast, agile horses rather than the heavy beasts of the dragoons or cuirassiers.

Personnel of the Second Combat Engineer Battalion assigned to the 2/8 are masters at construction and destruction. They clear mine fields or lay them, build simple bridges or blow big ones up.

A platoon from "Gusto," the Second Reconnaissance Battalion, provides reconnaissance for the BLT. These men are extensively trained and are expected to operate independently, often for days, in enemy territory, known as "Indian Country," observing and reporting. "Doomsday," one group, provided by the MEU to its BLT, provides extensive radio and communications support.

Aboard ship other Marines are easily identifiable by the distinctive black T-shirts imprinted with "Long Distance Death" that they wear as they run for miles around the flight deck. They are the battalion commander's Surveillance and Target Acquisition (STA) Platoon, an elaborate euphemism for snipers. Working in pairs and wearing improbable-looking Ghillie suits, they stalk the enemy with specially designed rifles. The suits, which provide almost perfect camouflage and resemble bushes, rocks, or hillsides, take many hours to make. They originated in Scotland where field hands would dress (as some still do) in such outfits to guard flocks of sheep against wolves and poachers. The entire platoon painstakingly works on constructing the Ghillie suits, which are a concoction of vanilla hemp rope strips, infrared-resistant netting, and assorted shades of burlap. The finished product weighs just under 20 pounds.

A reconnaissance team returns to the cavernous well deck of the USS *Nassau*.

A COMBAT RUBBER RAIDING CRAFT RAID

MISSION: NLT 2100 (LOCAL), Company E will conduct an RRC raid to destroy the terrorist base camp located in the vicinity of 860235, ensuring in the process that there is no collateral damage to local civilian property or injury to local civilian inhabitants.

Planning started early in the day, minutes after the mission was received. The intelligence officer reported that at base camp, which was close to the water, terrorists with speedboats were getting ready to attack a nearby U.S. freighter. About 30 terrorists were said to be present. "Rowdy's Raiders" were charged with collecting any enemy documents they could find and trying to capture a few of the terrorists for interrogation.

Some Marines were designated to bring along empty packs so that the documents could be collected quickly and stashed. The time ashore would be as short as possible, and the forces were to withdraw after the successful completion of the mission.

Reinforcement plans were worked out in the event that Rowdy ran into trouble. "Bald Eagle," defined by planners as a reinforced company, would stand by to be lifted in by helicopter or taken in by surface means at a moment's notice. "Sparrow Hawk" was defined as a reinforced platoon, to be similarly used.

Many hours after the sun had gone down, ten Rigid Raiders slid silently into the water, loaded with ten Marines each. The new moon was virtually invisible. The troops wore camouflage paint on their faces, black gloves, and "Mustang Suits," heavily insulated garments that could keep them floating for up to two hours in case of a mishap. On a beach not too far from the objective, they stopped, dropped their water survival gear, and then split up into two teams for the assault.

One unit landed a mile or so south of the objective while the other, five boats in all, held off. The team that landed first moved silently through woods and grass to be in position to attack the terrorist headquarters from one end. Precision timing was critical. As soon as the first group started attacking, the second landed a few yards from the terrorist camp and attacked from the other side.

I was inside the "terrorist camp" when the assault started. Our big campfire blazed brightly, illuminating our positions and killing our night vision. It was easy for the attacking force to take the terrorists out with well-aimed fire. Although I knew the plan, I was still surprised by the fast and furious attack. Smoke grenades, screams, camouflaged faces, and the rat-ta-tat-tat of automatic rifles firing reminded me of a scene from an adventure movie.

Military history shows that during most well-run surprise ambushes, the attackers almost never lose anybody, while those who are attacked suffer major losses. The proof of that lesson was evident as I watched the assault take place. The firefight was over within minutes.

Once the camp was secure, the attackers quickly fanned out, searching "dead" terrorists, collecting papers and weapons, and taking prisoner those who had been designated as enemies by the "play plan," myself included. Even though this was only a training exercise, we prisoners were treated roughly. I found myself being dragged to the stowed-away Rigid Raiders through cold water, my hands and feet bound by simple plastic handcuffs. Only after we had been heartily thrown into the bottoms of the boats were we released and the exercise declared complete.

Waiting for something to happen is one of the things Marines learn to live with.

CH-46 Sea Knights take off from a narrow airstrip at Camp Mosby in North Georgia. This landing strip is used primarily for night operations training.

(Above) Six AV-8B Harriers are assigned to an MEU. (Overleaf, pages 78-79) AH-1 Cobra attack helicopters support troop assaults. Equipped with rockets and missiles, they can escort troop-carrying helicopters to "hot" landing zones and suppress hostile fire.

such a job in a squadron dominated by helicopter pilots that I heard about it well before meeting the squadron. The squadron's intelligence officer was a Huey pilot; the logistics officer, a Cobra pilot; and the AMO (responsible for aircraft maintenance), a CH-53 Echo "driver."

The ACE provides the MEU (SOC) commander with a highly adaptable weapon. Virtually every mission can be fulfilled by the squadron. Combining aircraft flown by pilots who have gotten to know each other enables complex missions to be run without the need to get "strangers" involved.

It used to be common during a deployment that the Harrier pilots "first met the helo pilots when the ship pulled out into the Atlantic," said Major Mitchell, the executive officer of the squadron.

To see how all these assets work together, imagine a Tactical Recovery of Aircraft and Personnel (TRAP) mission. A U.S. Air Force reconnaissance jet has just made an emergency landing some 40 miles inland from the Libyan coast in a remote area not covered by Libyan radar. It is essential that the aircraft be destroyed and

that the pilot be recovered, because the "national command authority" (meaning the U.S. President) wants to avoid a hostage situation and the loss of vital intelligence. While it is in the recovering unit's favor that the Libyans are not yet alerted and that any Libyan forces are several hours away from the pilot's location, little time can be wasted. Marine forces, which have just completed an operation in Spain and are now sailing east in the Med, are alerted and ordered to recover the pilot and destroy the plane. After some deliberation, the MEU (SOC) commander orders the ACE commander to plan and execute the recovery mission. Because such operations have been planned and rehearsed before, all the ACE commander needs to do is adapt existing plans to the specifics of the situation, absorb the available intelligence, and proceed.

Six hours later as night comes and the moon starts rising, two Harriers launch and take positions "up top," ready to come to the aid of others in an instant. The remaining Harriers are on standby aboard the ship, which is about 30 miles off the Libyan coast and moving closer. Two CH-53 Echos take off next. Their pilots wear night-vision goggles, and within minutes they cross the beach over an unpopulated piece of land west of Tripoli. They are shadowed by the Harriers, which are well out of range of Libyan anti-aircraft fire. Close-in protection is provided by two AH-1T Cobra gunships that have launched and are now flying formation with them. The CH-53Es carry Force Reconnaissance Marines assigned by the MEU to the ACE. Midway between the ship and the coast, a Huey circles with the ACE commander aboard; he oversees this airborne command post and serves as a radio relay link between the raiding force and the reserves aboard ship (including the four Harriers and one reinforced infantry company that is ready to deploy on CH-46 helicopters in case of trouble).

The four helicopters enter Libyan airspace flying

low. Their pilots use their night-flying skills and the terrain for protection as they approach the crash site. One CH-53 helicopter lands. Marines deploy from it and set up a hasty defense, while a medic attends to the downed pilot, who has sustained several severe cuts on his leg. The second CH-53 stays airborne in case the Marines aboard are needed as reinforcements. The two Cobras remain on picket duty, hiding behind nearby dunes. Within ten minutes the thumbs-up is given, and the vital parts of the downed plane are destroyed. Additional explosive charges will be detonated as soon as the insertion force leaves. With the wounded pilot now on a stretcher safely inside its belly, the CH-53 takes off and joins the other helicopters as they make their way back to the safety of the ship. A total of 95 minutes has elapsed since the force left the ship, with just 15 of them spent on the ground.

SURVIVAL

Both helicopter-borne companies of the battalion have been trained in helicopter survival. While the training terrifies many, studies have shown that completion of the training dramatically increases the chances for survival in the event a helicopter goes down in the water (or "drink" as Marine pilots are fond of saying).

One helicopter-crash survival training center is located at the Marine Corps Air Station in Cherry Point, North Carolina. There, Marines learn how to keep a cool head under water. "Panic is 80 percent in the mind," instructors are fond of saying. The mental factor can be dealt with. What to do with the remaining 20 percent is the rough part.

Dressed up in flight suits, boots, life vests, and helmets, Marines begin training by learning how to

An AH-1 Cobra helicopter maneuvers over the water.

(Top) Formation flying is practiced frequently. This CH-53E follows closely behind another. (Bottom left) The cockpit of a helicopter is just as complex as that of a jet aircraft. (Bottom right) HMM-264 commander Lieutenant Colonel John G. ''Tennessee'' Castellaw, who was named Marine Aviator of the Year for 1989, and his deputy, the squadron's executive officer Major Hank ''Crank'' Mitchell, pose for the camera in front of their men and aircraft.

float with full gear on and how to inflate their vests.

Once they have mastered that skill, they head for the "helo dunker," a mocked-up helicopter fuselage that is part of a giant dunking machine. Marines in groups of six sit down in the mockup, memorize the nearest exit points, and assume the crash position—head down between the knees, arms wrapped around the legs. A switch is activated, and the fuselage plummets toward the water. Just before going under, the men take a final deep breath. As soon as the trainer hits the water, they count to 12 (the approximate time it takes the trainer to completely settle in the water) and then release their seatbelts and swim out of the nearest exit.

The next procedure is not so easy. This time when the Marine-filled fuselage enters the water, the drum spins a full 180 degrees to simulate a helicopter turning over in the water. After the 12 count, the Marines try to locate their exits in a world suddenly turned upside down. In the process they find themselves hitting and getting hit by the elbows, knees, and boots of their comrades, also anxiously seeking a way out. Panic, they try to remember, is 80 percent mental.

The final, most terrifying test is conducted while wearing goggles painted black. Once in the water, Marines are not only turned upside down, but they must blindly find their exits just like they would during a nighttime crash.

Pilots and crew chiefs also train with a small bottle of oxygen that gives them five extra minutes of air. The bottle is part of a survival vest. Ideally, all passengers would be issued the same survival gear as that worn by the air crew, but providing everyone with survival vests is impractical. Infantry units that fly on helicopters are already loaded down with 80 pounds or more of gear, including flak jackets, helmets, weapons, packs, and canteens. There is no way to add an additional 50-pound survival vest.

The helicopter crash training, which must be repeated every four years, is critical. "There are no second chances in a crash," instructors casually reminded their students. "No second chances."

(Above) "Yellow shirts" guide landing aircraft to the right spots on the tight flight deck. (Facing) CH-46 Sea Knights, with their rotary blades folded to conserve space, parked on the USS *Nassau* flight deck.

CARRIER LANDINGS

Marine pilots are trained to land on carriers, as well as on the postage-stamp-sized flight decks of frigates, destroyers, and supply ships. On the flight schedule, the landings are called "CQs" for "carrier quals," and pilots practice them day and night.

To a casual observer, such landings may look deceptively easy, especially if one merely admires the graceful movement of the helicopters as they settle into position on the flight deck. That grace hides the pilots' sweaty hands and intense concentration, the concern of the crew members, and the barely suppressed sighs of relief when the birds finally touch down, consistently hitting the bull's-eye.

Landing a helicopter at day or night on a ship deck means placing a 20,000-pound aircraft on a spot that

Landing on a pitching aircraft carrier requires close coordination between pilot, crew chief, and flight deck crew. (Above) Once this CH-46 Sea Knight lands ''on the dot,'' the flight deck crew runs to secure the helicopter with chains to the deck. (Facing) A UH-1N Huey crew chief gives his pilot a running report on the landing approach to the USS *Nassau*.

(Facing) Marines jog around CH-53E Super Stallions on the flight deck. (Below) The insignia patch of the MEU's composite air squadron.

offers only 10 feet of clearance from head to tail and that calls for the rear landing gear to be positioned three feet from the edge of the flight deck. This spot has been carefully prescribed to ensure that as many helicopters as possible can load or unload troops on deck.

While the flight deck appears to grow progressively larger to those whose feet pound it hard on early-morning conditioning runs, it seems to shrink for incoming pilots. Judging distances while airborne can be difficult. Stiff winds and sudden, pitching movements as the carrier rides the undulating ocean are other disadvantages for which pilots must compensate.

When a pilot returns to the ship, his landing becomes an elaborate team effort. First, a yellow-shirted Sailor on the flight deck gestures with his arms like a symphony conductor to signal the pilot into position.

Meanwhile, the helicopter's crew chief leans out of the port-side hatch and keeps up a running commentary on where the helicopter is hovering at every moment. The assistant crew chief, on the starboard side, peers out and makes sure that the landing gear has cleared the side of the ship.

Responding to the directions of the flight deck crew, as well as his own crew members, the pilot hovers, moving forward and sideways, all the while adjusting for any forward motion of the ship. At night, when visibility is limited, landing is even more difficult.

There are no creature comforts in the field. Meals come out of plastic pouches, crates serve as chairs, and vehicles provide shaving mirrors. Training is on-going, but for those not on duty, building brains is as important as building muscles. USMC Commandant A.M. Gray has put together a list of recommended books for officers and enlisted men, who are required to read several each year.

97

(Above) A lightly armed force can be inserted into enemy territory clandestinely with Rigid Raiders. (Facing) For more heavy, conventional assaults, Marines use Amtracs. The one shown here carries Amtrac Detachment commander Lieutenant K.S. Ralston.

The USS *Nassau*, a Landing Ship, Helicopter, Amphibious (LHA-4),
carries some 2,000 Marines on board.

CHAPTER 7 REVEILLE

MY ALARM WENT OFF at 0130 hours. After a quick shower, a rushed breakfast, and time out to fill two canteens with cold water and don a flak jacket, web gear, lifejacket, pack, and helmet, I lumbered forward in the ship to the acclimatization room.

There the rush stopped as I waited with the other Marines for our group, or "stick," to be loaded on a helicopter. All around me Marines were stretched out on the deck, leaning against exercise equipment, hanging their rifles and helmets from weight-lifting machines and assuming improbable positions as they tried to continue their sleep. Weapons were everywhere, and many served as pillows.

"Why do we always do this at night?" grumbled one veteran Marine. "People are supposed to sleep." But like the rest of us, he knows that night offers cover, protection.

The incessant roar of helicopters gearing up served as a reminder that an assault was about to commence. I groped in my pocket to find ear plugs to screen out the noise that would intensify once I got out on the flight deck and climbed aboard the camouflage-painted beast that would fly me ashore.

Finally, a Marine assigned to Combat Cargo called out our "serial." We followed him through a dark narrow passageway to a catwalk just below the flight deck. He held an oversized flashlight, known as a wand, which cast a subdued blue light over the night scene. Everything around us vibrated in the roar of the six helicopters overhead on the USS *Nassau* flight deck. Our CH-46 helo was located, and we rushed up a ladder to the flight deck to be greeted by hot engine blast. The flight deck itself was dark; all visible light had been extinguished or covered with a blue filter.

Once aboard our helo, we placed our packs in front of us, and the crew chief checked to see that everyone was strapped in. While we waited for the other aircraft to load and the ship's air boss to grant permission for takeoff, the squad leader signaled for us to rehearse the crash position. Then everybody pointed out the nearest exit.

At last the quality of the noise changed as the rotor pitch adjusted and the vibration levels went up. The ugly, noisy beast that was just moments ago chained to the flight deck took off, transformed from an ungainly aircraft to a bird with a hint of grace.

Our helicopter and the others, maybe 15 altogether, circled in a waiting pattern over the ships. On every rotation we were treated to the sight of a near-full moon that turned the silent waves into silver and cast a smooth light on the dark fleet. Some Marines fell asleep and began snoring and snorting. Others watched the crew chiefs who served as additional eyes for the pilots by keeping a careful look out for other helos.

After some 6,000 miles of sea voyage, the assault—a training operation on a Spanish beach—was on, and the helos headed toward the coastline, distinct in the moon's light. "Golf" Company, in the helos, was on its way to secure Landing Force Objective 2, a large mesa deeper inland that towered over the landing beach.

Below, LCUs and Amtracs kicked up salt-white spray as they streaked across the sea toward the beach they would soon secure. They were well aligned, one wave out in front, followed by a second and a third.

In preparation for this assault, Recon Marines and Navy SEALs had been inserted the night before by boat or parachute into the area of operation. The SEALs checked out the beach and radioed back to the ships information regarding any obstacles, the beach gradient, and suspected enemy concentrations so that the commanders aboard ship could adjust their plans accordingly. The Recon Marines moved inland—hopefully undetected—where they observed any activity and reported to their commanders on what

(Top) A helicopter sets down in a landing zone at night. (Bottom) This UH-1 Huey helicopter has been equipped with multiple radios preparatory to its role as airborne command post during an assault. In the center, Battalion Landing Team 2/8 commander Lieutenant Colonel Matthew Broderick listens to reports from his commanders on the ground.

they saw. Their job was to spot enemy troops and ensure that Marine assault forces did not land in the middle of a heavy concentration. They had discovered that the mesa was lightly defended.

A few minutes before the first amphibious wave hit the sand and disgorged fully armed Marines, the helos crossed the beach. They remained invisible to the enemy, flying nimbly between steep, rocky hills. Night-vision goggles produced green-tinted images of the terrain, allowing the pilots to perform as if it were daylight. They kept close to the surface, using the hills and cliffs as cover, keeping the telltale sounds of approaching helicopters from the enemy as long as possible.

Two Cobra gunships flew picket duty. Like angry wasps, they darted through the air in everything but a straight line to avoid ground fire. While this was only a practice assault, they flew like it was the real thing.

The helicopter pilots avoided landing on top of automobile-sized boulders that cluttered the landing zone. They did not, however, avoid the thicket of thorn bushes that covered the mesa. After they touched down, the Marines moved out silently. In less than 60 seconds, everyone had exited the helos and was well clear.

The helicopters took off and were swallowed by the darkness. The noise that had been with us for the past two hours disappeared, and I was startled by the silence. I sat down as best I could between the thorn bushes. Nearby Marines whispered curses as they got tangled in the thorns. My trousers become wet as they soaked up the plentiful dew all around us. Finally, using preplanned marching orders adjusted on the spot by the company commander, the platoon commanders, and the NCOs running their squads, the assault force slowly moved out across the mesa to engage the hostiles. No words were spoken. Hand signals were the only form of communication. Somewhere behind us the helicopters dropped off additional troops.

The sharp crack of machine gun blanks echoed in the distance, indicating that the first firefight of the day, which had yet to be greeted by the warming rays of the sun, was on. Within minutes, the Marines successfully defeated the unsuspecting hostiles, and Landing Force Objective 2 was declared secure.

"In real life," said one veteran, "it would take longer, but not that much."

Once again, surprise had carried the day.

THE MED

The practice assault on the Spanish beach marked the start of a month-long "float" to the Mediterranean, with other operations in Turkey, Sardinia, and Portugal; port calls in Monte Carlo, Naples, Haifa, and Lisbon; and an agonizing 35 days waiting off the coast of Beirut for something, anything, to happen.

The Mediterranean is one of the most likely battlegrounds for a MEU (SOC). Others include locations in the Pacific and off the coasts of South America, where interdicting drug traffic might become necessary, and Africa, where American lives were threatened in 1990 during the civil unrest in Liberia and the Iraqi invasion of Kuwait.

"You must remember that we do not come here on a training mission," said MEU commander Colonel John B. Creel of the Med. "This is a 'real world' mission, and we may be called upon to do our mission at any time."

His is not an idle claim. Since the Second World War, more than 260 incidents throughout the world have required the use of U.S. armed forces. Naval forces—in particular, aircraft carriers, amphibious ships, and Marines—have been the "force-of-choice" in more than 210 of these instances.

Pilots prepare for a mission in the ready room of the USS *Nassau*.

"They were there, and they were ready," explained a Marine officer.

Ever since the young U.S. republic dispatched a few wooden sailing ships to the coast of Libya in 1801, Marine Corps and Navy forces have been deployed to the Mediterranean to show the flag and sometimes put the "big stick" to work. Since 1948 Marines have been there continuously, guarding American interests. The mere presence of these forces, along with the Navy's fleets, are effective deterrents, but sometimes they do get used, as happened at Beirut in 1958, 1982-1984, and almost again in 1989.

BEIRUT

Beirut brings back painful memories for Marines and will continue to do so for a long time. On October 23, 1983, more than 200 of their comrades died in their sleep, blown up by a truck bomb driven by a Shiite terrorist. Those Marines who were in Beirut at that time feel personally responsible for the inability of the United States to succeed in keeping peace in the region.

"We were badly used in Beirut," said Marine Captain Joe Dowdy who served with U.S. forces in the Lebanese capital as a platoon commander.

Another Marine, frustrated by the hostages, hijackings, and bombings of American installations overseas, said, "You feel totally impotent here on ship with the best training and weapons the Corps has to offer. There seems to be nothing we can do."

"I get so angry when I think about this, I just start shaking," commented yet another, a sergeant from the Eighth Marines.

Marines always say that you should never forget the dead, except during a battle, when you should not think about them too much. "You can't remain effective," explained a Marine veteran of Vietnam. "It is only after it is all over that you have time to grieve."

One could sense the barely suppressed anger among the Marines in the first days of the "crisis" in August 1989. Hizballah, the "Party of God," a Shiite militia movement supported by Iran, threatened to execute one of their hostages, Marine Colonel William R. Higgins. In response, Sixth Fleet ordered the 26th MEU (SOC), then embarked on three Navy amphibious ships, to hold off the coast of Lebanon. Hizballah's threat came in retaliation to an Israeli kidnapping of a key Hizballah leader. Two days after the threat was issued, Hizballah distributed a videotape showing the execution of Colonel Higgins; the unit's stay off the coast of Lebanon was extended indefinitely. Most of

Sixth Fleet was ordered to wait off the shores of Beirut. A threat to execute a second hostage further intensified the crisis. At the same time fighting in Lebanon increased tremendously, with an implied threat to the U.S. Embassy there.

Early on in the crisis, I had a long talk with the battalion commander about Lebanon. We shared our anger and frustration about the apparent inability of the United States to deal effectively with the problems in that country.

"Those peoples' logic is not our western logic, and whatever we do seems wrong," he said. "The emotional response to go in and blow up a bunch of things is not necessarily the best course."

For some Marines this fact is hard to accept, because the people who killed Colonel Higgins probably belong to the same terrorist group that destroyed the Marine barracks in Beirut in 1983.

During the 35 days spent steaming in a circle off Lebanon, the atmosphere became more purposeful on board ship. Routine plans were reevaluated to be ready to meet any contingency. Countless meetings took place, many doors stayed closed, and signs were posted proclaiming certain areas of the ship off limits for those without a secret clearance.

"We are drowning in work," said one of the MEU's intelligence officers.

How were the Marines to be put to use if called to action in Beirut? At first nobody knew. Then, during the first few days of the crisis, possible missions became known. One involved standing by to rescue pilots who might be shot down if the U.S. President went ahead with the major airstrike that seemed likely in the event that the second hostage was killed. Another mission involved supporting possible rescue attempts to free the remaining hostages. The most likely mission, evacuating the U.S. Embassy, dominated preparations.

A big blackboard in the battalion commander's

stateroom listed four options for the potential evacuation. Each detailed the "commander's intent," advantages and disadvantages, and the likely conditions under which such an option would be used. At first glance it looked like the blackboard back at the North Carolina training center. But our location and an enormous black-and-white photograph of the embassy compound served as stark reminders that this blackboard was deadly serious. As an observer I was cautioned repeatedly to keep my mouth shut. "It could kill a lot of people if details become known," said the battalion commander.

Months later, these options remain confidential. One day Marines may be called on again to evacuate the U.S. embassy in Beirut. Nobody knows for sure.

Watching the planning process, I saw the purpose of the predeployment training. Yet even with all the previous rehearsals, I could tell that the planning was rough for the senior officers and those with jobs in intelligence or operations. The strain of preparing, revising, waiting, and briefing was visible on their faces, in their gestures, and in their voices, which were just a bit sharper, shorter, more severe.

On the second day off Beirut, the USS *Nassau* moved at "flank speed" to the coast of Sicily, where we waited for the arrival of two high-speed HH-53D Air Force helicopters that were being flown in from Germany. Their estimated arrival time changed constantly. The delay, as reports had it, was occasioned by the French, who refused to grant overflight rights to the two aircraft. Without such rights, the helos would have had to fly around Spain and Portugal to get to Italy. Fortunately, the French relented, and the Air Force helos made it to the *Nassau* about 48 hours after our arrival. They were to be used for Combat Search and Rescue (CSAR) in the event a plane got shot down over Lebanon. They were also needed as support in case of an airstrike. HH-53D helicopters

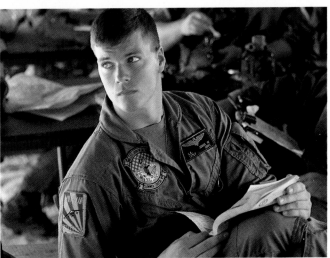

Both grunts and pilots receive extensive briefings before a mission to ensure that they know what will happen and what their specific jobs will be. (Top) A platoon commander aboard the USS *Barnstable County* briefs his troops. (Bottom) A Harrier pilot listens to the specifics of his mission to support ground operations. (Overleaf, pages 106-107) AV-8B Harriers lined up on the flight deck of the USS *Nassau*.

carry secret high-tech avionics packages and specialized equipment that enable them to do things Marine Corps helos cannot.

One morning while waiting off Sicily, an insistent tap on my shoulder woke me up at about 0400 hours. "Sir, the colonel wants you to be on the flight deck at 0500," a Marine pilot whispered to me.

"Why?"

"We are launching two 53s and some Harriers on a special mission."

A CH-46 Sea Knight resupplies the USS *Nassau*. An amphibious task force can sustain itself almost indefinitely with supplies brought in by other ships.

I got up, trying not to disturb the chaplain and the doc, but the chaplain woke and asked, "Has something happened?"

"I don't know," I replied. After grabbing my life vest and helmet, I left and made my way up to the flight deck triage room, where by 0530 hours members of the Force Recon Detachment, men from 2nd ANGLICO, special communications people, and others were waiting under the watchful eyes of the MEU's operations officer, Lieutenant Colonel Rueger.

Everyone was all packed, complete with rifles, pistols, and radios, to fly some 725 miles across the Mediterranean to the USS *Shreveport* for a CSAR mission likely that day. It would be a long flight for the helos, even with aerial refueling, but the Marines had to go because the Air Force was still stuck in diplomatic tangles with the French. The sun was just rising above the horizon when the group traversed the almost empty flight deck in one long line, heads down as if to counterbalance the weight of their packs

and to shield their eyes from the hot engine blast. The few who had come to see them off had that look in their eyes of, "Oh, if only I could go with you."

The two CH-53 Echos took off from the *Nassau* and flew across the Mediterranean, refueling once in mid-air. Their flight was protected along the way by Harriers that had been armed with Sidewinder missiles. After landing on the *Shreveport*, the Marines learned that President George Bush had called off the CSAR mission. The troops flown to the *Shreveport* in such a great rush were never used.

During our stay off Lebanon, some of the Navy people aboard ship voiced concern about small boat attacks and other low-tech attempts to blow us out of the water. As a precaution, the USS *Nassau* frequently practiced its guns, including the Close-In Weapon System (CIWS), a computerized gun that can fire off 3,000 rounds per minute. The Harriers and Cobras were also armed during all daylight hours.

Resupply became necessary. One morning, we took on more than one million gallons of fuel and some 200,000 gallons of jet fuel for the helicopters. We also received vital stores. These were flown on from the tanker and supply ships that pulled up alongside the USS *Nassau* during an Underway Replenishment, or UNREP as the Navy calls it. In this amazing process, the *Nassau* and the supply ship steamed slowly side by side and transferred fuel while helicopters shifted stores such as flour and spare parts, apple juice and lubricants, frankfurters and medical items. It is said that the U.S. Navy is the only master of this difficult art, which allows a fleet to stay out indefinitely, independent of ports and bases.

Rumors on board ship are a wonderful thing. They occupy the mind and provide endless raw material for heated debate. News from the outside world is exceptionally sparse and available only to a few, such as commanders and intelligence officers. The rest must rely on snippets of information and the occasional letter from home. These little bits of information, coupled with the imaginations of ship-bound men, become the foundation of many rumors. Some Marines start rumors just to test how long it will take for the rumor to circulate and return, but like all such sports, there are limits to the game, and rumors generally die quickly, to be replaced by new ones. A few of the hardier rumors will spill over the ship's side and make their way to other ships in the fleet. There, they are often improved and modified before returning to their place of origin a few days later. Such rumors are taken more seriously because they come from the outside world and have demonstrated their strength by making the treacherous journey from ship to ship.

One day we went over to the USS *Iowa* and watched her shoot her 5-inch guns. She didn't fire the 16-inch guns to the disappointment of her visitors. The captain of the *Iowa* was reported by his crew to be "steaming with anger" that he was not allowed to sail close to Beirut and add some visual presence to our mission. Most of the fleet was located 100 miles or so off the Lebanese coast.

While we were there, we watched the *Iowa* launch a Remotely Piloted Vehicle (RPV), which resembles a large toy airplane and is designed to fly some 80 miles or so in front of the battleship. Video cameras inside the RPV transmit a steady stream of pictures back to the ship. Next to invisible to radar, it marries World War II technology with the very best of the late twentieth century. RPVs are an essential tool in the special-operations bag of tricks. Marines use them as "spies" to check out landings, adjust artillery fire, collect intelligence, or monitor developing situations. Its return to the ship was unglamorous at best. After an elegant pass over the *Iowa*, the RPV flew straight into an enormous net at the aft of the ship and collapsed like a tangled bird.

(Top) The USS *Iowa* supports an amphibious landing with fire from its 5-inch guns. (Bottom) A Remotely Piloted Vehicle is launched from the USS *Iowa*. With on-board video cameras, this small aircraft can record the impact of the ship's batteries or the progress of an amphibious landing without endangering the life of a pilot.

(Clockwise from center left) Marines train for close combat, inspect their rifles, stay in top condition with daily runs around the flight deck, sleep in tight quarters aboard ship, and await mail from home, which arrives in large orange bags.

Back on the USS *Nassau*, not a day went by without a rehearsal or test. Some were as simple as seeing how many people could be squeezed into a CH–53E helicopter or how quickly it could be loaded with equipment. At times five or more helicopters flew around all night testing flight plans over the water. Virtually none of the options and methods were new; all of them had been practiced before.

Apart from staff officers of the MEU command element, the squadron worked the longest hours, planning and training. Crew chiefs, refuelers, combat cargo personnel, young Marines working in flight equipment and aircraft maintenance, all labored without stop. The pilots too talked about the strain of long days. In his daily talk, late at night, the captain reported that the *Nassau* had some 5,000 takeoffs and landings in August alone, compared to 5,000 during the first two months of the float combined.

It was meant to cheer when the chaplain reminded us that it could be much worse. Just one year before, he said, he had spent 97 days aboard ship in the Indian Ocean. That length of time, we quickly figured, translated into four cans of beer, because Navy regulations allow each man two cans of beer after every 45 days of continuous sea duty.

Maintaining morale during our five weeks off Lebanon in what the Navy calls MODLOC or Miscellaneous Operational Details, Local Operations, was a challenge. One day the ship held a "steel-beach picnic." Hot dogs and burgers were served on the black flight deck, which was unbearably hot under the blazing August sun.

Early in the crisis, the Sixth Fleet started to receive mail in orange bags that cluttered the triage room on the flight deck. Mail call is one of the best times aboard ship, and the importance of receiving mail increased as the likelihood of making phone calls diminished. Those who didn't get any mail were pitied; those who got care packages from home were eyed jealously. Some received homemade cookies and shared freely. One of my roommates, the doc, got a five-pound box of party mix. Someone else got fancy jams. Everything was treasured because many items were hard, if not impossible, to get on ship. Resupplies of socks and other utilitarian items were also much appreciated.

Mail is a great morale booster, and the Navy does a great job getting it to Sailors and Marines no matter where they are located. During the crisis, the USS *Nassau* became a mail center for the rest of the Sixth Fleet, and tons of mail passed over its flight deck.

Chaplain Lou Iasiello, a Franciscan with six years in the Navy, also attempted to maintain morale, and his prayers were eagerly awaited:

"Lord,
 Things are sort of dragging
And we've all caught MODLOC blues;
Traveling in circles
Gives our lives a darkened hue.
 We need a boost to lift us up
And push us towards the sky;
To lighten all our weary hearts
We'll give anything a try.
 So fill us Lord with special strength
And lead us through the night,
Till liberty is sounded
With Haifa's Hills in sight."

Despite everyone's best efforts to keep spirits high, at times a sense of uselessness hung in the air. There is a limit to how many people can wash laundry, scrub decks, work in the messhalls, or clean weapons. The flight schedule was so heavy that even the time for physical training on the flight deck was severely restricted.

Young lieutenants occupied themselves by sitting in the wardroom lounge and swapping ideas on what else could be done to keep the Marines busy. Their

The Black Knights squadron designs special cruise patches for each deployment.

task was not easy. Some 1,200 energetic young men—averaging nineteen years of age—were essentially being confined to a space that would make an overcrowded jail look spacious. It was hot aboard the *Nassau*, the air conditioning was undependable, and tempers flared easily. How to tire the young Marines out, make them feel useful, was the subject of much discussion.

Daydreams were one way to wile away the time. "Where will I go when I get back?" some wondered. "What will my child look like?" "Will my wife really want to go on a week long cruise?"

One night in the officers mess, several lieutenants talked about their sons and about how much they hoped to see them follow in their footsteps. "I can't wait to see him in uniform," one said. "It's a given. My first born will go into the Corps. It's tradition." That none of them had children and only one was married did not detract from the realism of their dreams, freely shared over a cup of weak Navy coffee.

Letter writing was another pastime, but occasionally complaints were received from parents whose sons hadn't written home.

"I will make him write," the battalion commander said when he heard one parent's complaint. "He will have no choice but to write. I will assign a senior to him to watch him at all times and make sure he writes. They'll watch him until he puts a letter into the mail box."

As the Marine's squad leader put it, "He don't write; he don't eat."

The platoon commander of the combat engineers, Lieutenant Jansen, tried to help in his own way. By hand and over many nights he wrote individual letters to the wives or parents of each of his 45 Marines. He did this several times during the deployment.

On September 7, 1989, the U.S. Embassy in Beirut, Lebanon, was evacuated without us. At the time of the evacuation, the USS *Nassau* and the other ships carrying Marine forces in the Mediterranean were in Naples on liberty. Embassy personnel flew out on their own Black Hawk helicopters. All along that method had been envisioned as the first evacuation option, and the Marines and other forces would have only come into play if the embassy had been under attack.

(Clockwise from top left) A cook stirs dinner for 2,000 Marines, while elsewhere Marines attend yet another briefing, practice marksmanship by firing off the bow of a ship, inspect weapons in the hangar bay of the USS *Nassau*, and share a ''spacious'' stateroom.

(Clockwise from top left) A Marine scrubs his helicopter to prevent corrosion from salty water and air; others clean their weapons, practice firing a .50-caliber machine gun, share a few moments of quiet conversation, and look on as Lieutenant Colonel John G. Castellaw promotes a young Marine of HMM-264. (Facing) Trailed here by the USS *Barnstable County*, the USS *Nassau* is the scene of intensive physical training.

CHAPTER 9 COMING HOME

MEMORIES OF DEPLOYMENTS last a lifetime. Yet to some Marines, the memories are marred by nightmares of how their marriages were torn apart during the long separations.

"I have done this six times," said one squadron master sergeant of his deployments, "and you just don't get used to it. It's hard on the wife and kids over and over again."

Married men and those in strong relationships "pay a heavy price for these deployments," the chaplain told me. "Judging by past experiences, I predict 40 divorces resulting from this deployment." Forty represents a full ten percent of the married men in the battalion. The chaplain's figure doesn't include the many men with girlfriends and common-law wives.

From its beginnings at Morehead City, North Carolina, this deployment showed telltale signs of being a typical float. Sitting in his spacious shipboard cabin, the battalion commander eyeballed a chart listing nine unauthorized absences, broken down by company and detachment. Young Marine lieutenants responsible for the actions of their absent men began to tell familiar stories to the commanding officer.

"Two wives tried to commit suicide (official naval language is that they displayed 'suicide gestures') to prevent their husbands from going away," one lieutenant reported.

For many young Marines this deployment is the first long trip away from home, and that, along with adapting to life aboard ship, is tough. A surprising number of them are married and have children.

I saw their families one sunny day before the deployment at Camp Lejeune, North Carolina. There, more than 600 Marines, Sailors, wives, and children attended "Family Day," an event held for the members and dependents of the 26th MEU. As has become custom, deploying units spend part of their predeployment work-up helping families to minimize the burdens of separation. This follows the oft-repeated guidance by Marine Corps Commandant General A.M. Gray to "take care of your own."

Family Day was a grand affair. The battalion displayed a variety of small weapons, howitzers, rubber boats, and light armored vehicles to show the families the types of equipment that Marines worked around all day. Some Marines played ball with the kids, while others set up pony rides, applied camouflage paint, and handed out 130-page coloring books called *Daddy's Days Away.*

"It makes you feel a little bit better," said one wife, who was attending the standing-room-only gathering with her husband, three-year-old son, and an additional child obviously on the way, "but it still doesn't do much to ease the emotional burden."

During Family Day speakers from the American Red Cross, the Jacksonville Police Department, the Navy Relief Society, the Camp Lejeune Provost Marshal's Office, the Family Service Center, and other agencies described the specific support services available to dependents.

A shadow battalion of "Key Wives" were on hand. "Commanded" by the wife of the commanding colonel, Key Wives are organized in a tight group to give each other support, pass the word, advise the younger ones, and somehow offer a tangible safety net.

Another critical link is the Dependent Affairs During Deployment (DADD) Coordinator. This member of the battalion stays behind and provides a day-to-day link with the deployed unit. Among other things, he deals with expired ID cards for dependents so that they can continue to shop at the PX.

"We want them to know they will be taken care of," said Colonel Matthew E. Broderick. "Family separations are never easy, but the months ahead can be much easier with the various supports available."

For some, the support apparently isn't enough. Thirty minutes past midnight one evening during the deployment, there was a knock on the stateroom door that I shared with the chaplain and the doc. A young platoon commander, holding on tightly to a message, looked for the chaplain, now awakened from his sleep.

"This just came in, Sir," the lieutenant told him. "This Marine's wife just packed up and left, and the children are still there. Social Services is taking care of them. Could you talk to him?"

For six months I shared a stateroom with the chaplain, and I saw the many problems caused by family separations. The urgent Red Cross message, the "Dear John" letter were almost daily events.

"Now is the time in the deployment when many marriages break up, when the wives just leave and go home to their parents," the chaplain said two months before our return home. "They've just had enough."

There is little a Marine on deployment can do about family crises that occur while he's away. Marines may go home only for the funerals of immediate family members. Since everyone aboard ship has a specific job that might be needed in the event of an emergency, the commander is understandably reluctant to let people go lest it diminish his combat power.

Confronted with all the problems of marriages between young and often inexperienced people, some in the Corps would like to see a return to the days when marrying before making sergeant was either disallowed or required a commander's permission. While not legal, such restrictions did save much heartache, according to those who have been in the Corps for 20 years or more.

A family reunites after six months' separation.

HOMECOMING

Homecoming is sweet for most, and the Navy attempts to ease the process of reuniting with families by helping the men adjust. It is "a process that may take another six months for some," said one member of the Return and Reunion Team on the USS *Nassau* as she crossed the Atlantic on her way home.

The Return and Reunion Team had joined the ship in its last port in the Med. This Navy-sponsored group is designed to deal head-on with the many problems of return. Wives back in the states attend similar meetings.

The team of three consisted of two Navy wives who worked in the Norfolk Navy family center and one Virginia state trooper. The trooper talked about drunk driving, changes in traffic rules, and tried to "basically get the kids, everybody, focused on being careful."

"For many," Trooper Bill Shell said, "their car is their proudest possession. They haven't driven in six months, and as soon as they get back, many of them will go on a long, long drive—to see parents, loved ones. They are all charged up and take crazy risks. I have had to deliver the word many times that a kid wouldn't be coming home."

The wives' talks were more delicate, some of them eliciting what can only be described as male giggling from the listeners. "Reestablishing intimacy" was one topic that was practically mandatory for all married men on the ship. Plenty of good advice was circulated, such as "let the wife drive the car for a few days; accept that the kids will quickly be critical, saying annoying things such as 'but mommy does it differently...'; accept decisions made in your absence, such as if your wife bought the wrong tires for the car."

A ship about to make port after a long deployment is a surreal place. All of us—and that included key people like the battalion commander—suddenly found ourselves cleaning floors and dusting behind bunks, ledges, and light fixtures. The Navy wanted a clean ship.

Boxes, stacked up everywhere, were strapped onto pallets, ready for loading onto helicopters and into boats. And seabags. I have never seen so many seabags tucked into such tight spaces before.

The goal was to be able to unload everything belonging to the MEU, the BLT, the squadron, and the logistics group in a day or less. When the Marines had deployed six months before, they had taken all their earthly possessions, leaving nothing behind but empty desks. Now they had to remove all that they'd brought along from the ship.

"We packed like we wouldn't return," said the BLT's Sergeant Major Kane.

Not all homecomings are as happy as this one. Long separations caused by deployments take their toll on relationships.

On the last night of the deployment, no one slept. "It's like the night before Christmas," said one eighteen-year-old Marine.

"Channel Fever," the chaplain called it.

The ship's television ran movies all night, and the squadron commander went to great lengths to impress on everybody that safety was still paramount and not to get carried away in the excitement.

Finally, the ship docked, and the unloading of people and equipment began. It was conducted by unit and roughly in the same order in which the units had been loaded. Most Marines got their first view of the shore from helicopters and landing crafts, because the flight deck had been closed for flight operations. Senior officers disembarked last, turning the ship back over to the Navy.

On shore, there were heartfelt embraces, enthusiastic handshakes, and few truly dry eyes (Marines don't cry, officially) as the newly ashore Marines reunited with hundreds of family members and friends who had come to welcome them home. With haunted looks, some Marines tried to spot the face of a wife who they knew was not there. Others met their new children for the first time. One young Marine, in particular, walked past with a new daughter that he would not relinquish. "It makes it all worthwhile, all ..." he said, as he proudly showed off the child in his arms.

Rigid Raiders approach a beach for an assault.

APPENDIX A MEU (SOC) MISSIONS

MISSIONS ARE TO THE MILITARY what job descriptions and assignments are to the civilian world. The MEU (SOC) concept, for the first time in many years, brings up to date the list of various jobs the unit is expected to be able to perform.

Each deployed MEU (SOC) trains for a set of 18 specific missions that reflect the uncertain political climate of the last years of the twentieth century. Large-scale combat operations are seen as less likely than nighttime raids, the evacuation of civilians, or protecting merchant ships from modern-day pirates.

The MEU is expected to be able to conduct several of these missions simultaneously or combine several missions into one operation. Each mission must be custom tailored to the specific situation, and ideally, each should be conducted under the protective cloak of darkness. Most importantly, the MEU must be ready to begin execution of the mission within six hours of receiving the order.

The **Amphibious Raid** is the cornerstone of the MEU job description. Each MEU is expected to be able to conduct a raid, be it by day or night, and do so with lightning speed. An amphibious raid could be used, for instance, to seize an airfield near coastal waters that will then be used to evacuate civilians (another MEU mission).

A typical **Limited Objective Attack** mission would involve a brief assault on one sector held by opposing forces, while the main mission or attack takes place elsewhere. The purpose of the mission is to spoil the enemy forces' setup and create chaos by drawing those forces away from the main area of operations.

As Marines in the 26th MEU pointed out, a **Noncombatant Evacuation Operation (NEO)** is the most likely mission an MEU can expect to conduct. In an NEO civilians would be evacuated from a combat zone or potentially life-threatening environment. Throughout its history, the Marine Corps has conducted many such operations, including coming to the aid of civilians in Peking (1899-1900), Saigon (1975), Beirut (1958, 1982, 1983), and Liberia (1990). Since an MEU is "forward deployed," to use Marine Corps lingo, it is immediately available to support such operations where, with the aid of helicopters and under a protective infantry screen, civilians are removed to the safety of nearby ships. Cobra attack helicopters and Harrier jump jets, both within an MEU's inventory, can provide a protective air screen and offer the ground commander access to almost "instant" close air support.

The Show of Force is one of the oldest naval missions and is often known as "Battleship Diplomacy." The Marine Corps can exert psychological pressure on another country just by showing up off its coast. The unit could, for example, conduct a "turn-away landing," an amphibious landing stopped just a few hundred yards from the beach. Jets and helicopters can fly by, and U.S. Navy ships supporting the Marines can attempt to look menacing. Except for when it uses its four battleships, however, the Navy is finding it increasingly difficult to "threaten" hostile shores with the mere presence of ships. To the untrained observer, modern ships appear to be devoid of any significant weapons, when in fact the missiles they carry make them extraordinarily lethal.

Reinforcement Operations are another specific mission. Typical examples would find Marines fast-roping onto the deck of a merchant ship in need of protection, a unit flying in to protect an airfield from insurgents, or forces being reinforced by Marines during combat.

Under the label **Security Operations** fall missions such as providing beefed-up security for embassies abroad. The ill-fated multinational peace-keeping mission in Lebanon in 1982-84 is representative of this type of mission.

As an extension of a show of force and as an instrument of foreign policy, **Training** of foreign military units is another mission. During and after every exercise, whether it be held in France, Italy, Portugal, Thailand, or Kenya, Marines can be found training with local units. The MEU has what are called "Mobile Training Units," which during predeployment are taught how to train others. The U.S. Navy often gets involved by providing their ships for additional training.

Civil Actions, like training, help build or reinforce favorable relationships between the United States and other countries. This mission can include medical or dental services for local populations or agricultural and community improvements. In 1988, for instance, the logistics support unit of the 26th MEU, the MSSG, helped build roads and bridges in Spain. MEUs also commonly become involved with charitable organizations in a host country.

Deception Operations have long been considered critical. To be effective an MEU should be expert in conducting feints, ruses, and decoys to confuse an enemy. Such operations would be typically conducted in support of another mission.

Fire Support Coordination is considered an essential mission for an MEU. Although limited in size, an MEU has access to substantial fire support, whether through its own artillery, Cobra gunships, Harrier jump jets, or naval gunfire from nearby Navy ships (including an occasional battleship).

Counterintelligence is a term that in the case of the MEU covers a host of activities, from efforts to defeat the work of hostile intelligence services to an aggressive effort to collect information on potential terrorists.

Initial Terminal Guidance is a mission designed to support another. It would entail, for instance, the nighttime insertion on a beach of a small team that would be equipped with a radio direction finder and other gear in order to guide approaching boats to shore safely. It could also be used while making a landing zone to guide helicopters into place or support parachute operations.

"A highly technical mission, **Signal Intelligence/ Electronic Warfare (SIGINT/EW)** calls for the MEU to collect and monitor electronic signals that can be interpreted and used to provide a commander with solid intelligence. SIGINT/EW is also used to jam a hostile force's communications system while defeating such jamming from opposing forces.

The **Tactical Recovery of Aircraft, Equipment, and Personnel (TRAP)** is a major MEU mission. It calls for high speed and versatility.

Clandestine Recovery Operations is another mission. In a hypothetical example where a pilot of a U.S. Air Force reconnaissance jet bails out over a hostile nation, Marines would be instructed to bring him back alive without the nation involved knowing about it.

It is likely that future combat will take place primarily in urban or populated areas. Accordingly, **Military Operations in Urban Terrain (MOUT)** is given high training priority. Portions of the MEU typically train in major U.S. cities, learning from local police departments or the Federal Bureau of Investigation. Among other activities, the training includes tasks such as shutting down power plants, clearing buildings, or landing helicopters on top of high-rise buildings or in tight urban parking lots.

Specialized Demolition Operations involve "blowing up" difficult targets. In April 1988 an actual demolition operation was conducted in the Persian Gulf by an MEU that destroyed some Iranian oil rigs. The Marines in the Gulf were required to detonate the oil rigs in such a way that no environmental damage from oil spills would take place, making the placement

The CH-46 helicopter is the primary troop lift airplane of the Marine Corps.

of explosives substantially more complicated.

Many Marines say that an **In Extremis Hostage Rescue** is the least likely mission they will be called upon to undertake. It is also the toughest one for which they train. Despite the low odds that Marines will ever participate in hostage rescues, there are powerful arguments for ensuring that Marine Corps units deployed in the Med, the Persian Gulf, or the Indian Ocean possess the expertise and training to conduct

such operations. It is well known that American hostages held captive in Lebanon since 1985 are moved frequently. If by chance their latest locations were to become known, rapid action would be necessary to exploit the opportunity to rescue them. Other U.S. special forces, such as the Army's Delta Force, would take too long to arrive at the location, sacrificing in the delay an opportunity that might not come again.

M101A1 105mm Howitzer and CH-53E Super Stallion.

APPENDIX B TOOLS OF THE TRADE

IN THE 1980S THE U.S. MARINE CORPS equipped itself with a wide range of new weapons and systems. Probably never before in the Corps' history, and particularly during peacetime, has there been such a wholesale acquisition of weapon systems.

Since 1983 all weapons in ground units, except for the M60 machine gun, the 105mm howitzer, and the Amtrac (AAV), have been replaced. Newly acquired weapons include the Squad Automatic Weapon (SAW), a potent, fully automatic 5.56mm machine gun; the Light Armored Vehicle; the 155mm howitzer; an improved model of the M16 rifle; a new 9mm automatic pistol to replace the venerable (and heavier) .45; new multipurpose vehicles such as the HMMWV (which replaced the Jeep); new grenade launchers; and more.

A glossary containing key weapons, equipment, skills, and designations used by a typical MEU (SOC), MEB, or MEF follows:

A-6 Intruder An all-weather, night-attack aircraft, the A-6 has excellent slow-flying capabilities as well as a speed of 685 mph at sea level. It has comprehensive navigation, radar, and attack systems and can carry up to 15,000 pounds of bombs. The A-6 Intruder is deployed with MEBs and MEFs.

AH-1T/W Cobra Attack power comes from the Cobra, the AH-1T/W assault helicopter. With its streamlined, four-foot-wide-fuselage, the AH-1T/W can hide behind a mountain, tree line, or in a shallow valley and then quickly pull up, advance, and fire. The Cobra's lethal arsenal includes 2.75-inch folding-fin aerial rockets or 5-inch "Zuni" rockets, TOW anti-tank missiles, AIM-9 missiles, bombs, and a 20mm Gatling gun. The AH-1T model can move at speeds of up to 170 knots and, with an auxiliary tank, stay in the air for a little more than three hours. The new AH-1W model, introduced to the Corps in the early 1990s, flies at a higher speed and carries more weapons.

AH-1 Cobra.

Air Naval Gunfire Liaison Company (ANGLICO) When attached to an MEU, ANGLICO's primary mission is to provide air or naval gunfire support to U.S. armed services and U.S. allies.

Amphibious Task Force (ATF) Generic term for the naval, landing, and air forces involved in an amphibious operation. Marines deployed to the Persian Gulf in 1990 traveled as part of one large ATF, consisting of more than 40 ships.

Amtrac See Assault Amphibious Vehicle

AN/PVS-5 An older-model night-vision system, the AN/PVS-5 contains second-generation image-intensifier tubes. AN/PVS-5s are used exclusively by ground forces; modified versions are used for aviation training.

AN/PVS-6 To meet the unique requirements of pilots, the Aviator's Night Vision Imaging System (ANVIS) was built using the AN/AVS-6 night-vision goggle, which features third-generation image-intensifier tubes. Because of their lighter weight (about 454 grams), AN/AVS-6s are more comfortable and balance more easily on a flight helmet, thus greatly reducing pilot fatigue.

Artillery An MEU will typically travel with two types of howitzers: the M101A1 105mm howitzer of

AT4 Anti-Tank Weapon.

World War II design and the modern towed M198 155mm howitzer, which was first fired in anger in Beirut in 1983. Larger MEUs would also be equipped with two types of self-propelled howitzers: the 8 inch and the 155mm. Marine Corps artillery personnel can make use of "smart ammunition" introduced in the 1980s, such as the Copperhead, which is guided to the target with the help of a laser. MEBs and MEFs will travel with additional artillery, such as 8-inch guns.

Assault Amphibious Vehicle (AAV) The Assault Amphibious Vehicle, better known as an Amtrac, is a heavily armored personnel carrier that can bring some 20 combat-equipped Marines from ship to shore. AAVs float and move in the water at speeds of up to nine knots; on land they move at substantially higher speeds. The Corps uses two types: the LVTP-7, which carries troops, and the LVTC-7, which is equipped to act as a command and control vehicle.

AT4 Anti-Tank Weapon A small weapon, the AT4 fires an 84mm M136 High Explosive Anti-Tank (HEAT) cartridge across distances of up to 2,100 meters, with a maximum effective range of 300 meters. It can penetrate 18 inches of steel.

Aviation Combat Element (ACE) The reinforced helicopter squadron, aircraft group, or aircraft wing assigned to an MEU (SOC), MEB, and MEF, respectively.

AV-8B Harrier An MEU's fixed-wing component normally consists of six AV-8B Harriers. These "jump jets" give the unit an air-strike and additional close-air-support capability. Equipped with a wide range of ordnance from Sidewinder air-to-air missiles to a 25mm Gatling gun, the Harrier can take on other aircraft at 550 knots, protect amphibious ships, and most importantly, support the assault force on the beach or deep inland. A new version entering service is equipped with a night-vision system, which allows the plane to operate in darkness, the preferred time for special operations.

Bald Eagle Code name for a reinforced Marine rifle company, which can be lifted by helicopter to support any element of an MEU. In a typical operation, a Bald Eagle stands by on ship or in a beachhead area and is ready to deploy in minutes to support a raid. A smaller version, a reinforced rifle platoon, is known as Sparrowhawk.

Battalion Landing Team (BLT) In amphibious operations, an infantry battalion reinforced by combat and service elements; the basic assault unit.

Battery Computer System (BCS) The high-tech BCS allows a commander to get much shorter response time and increased accuracy of artillery fire from the battery of howitzers. Introduced to the Corps in the late 1980s, the device performs all computations for fire missions and interfaces with radio equipment for digital communications. This versatile system can run three regular missions and two special missions simultaneously, keeping track of 12 howitzers, 60 targets, and various other factors. "It replaces a lot of manual calculations," said one artillery lieutenant. "I would think it doubled if not tripled our response rate."

Brigade Service Support Group (BSSG) The support arm of an MEB responsible for logistics.

Carrier Qualifications (CQs) The designation for aircraft carrier landings on a flight schedule.

CH-46 Sea Knight Combat tested in Vietnam, Grenada, and Beirut, the CH-46 is a true veteran. It is not uncommon to see a crew chief born in 1971 working on a helicopter built in 1967. Pilots flying the aircraft (known as "Frogs") are more commonly associated with Marine Corps air forces than with any other branch of armed services. Part of their job, perhaps their most important one, is flying grunts from the safety of ships or the rear into a landing zone (LZ) far forward. In some squadrons you will see CH-46s with patches covering bullet holes that were received while landing in a "hot" LZ. CH-46s can carry 25 Marines or, when carrying an internal fuel tank, 10 troops. They can also carry 4,200 pounds of cargo, such as pallets of supplies or any combination of two jeeps or trailers. Externally, it can carry loads weighing in excess of 5,000 pounds.

Range is the CH-46's major limitation. The helicopter's combat radius under good conditions is only about 75 nautical miles, which limits its usefulness in special-operations missions. When equipped with internal fuel tanks, radius increases by some 45 nautical miles. Maximum speed is 145 knots, with a 100-120-knot cruising speed. CH-46s can be armed with two .50-caliber heavy machine guns. The V-22 Osprey is intended to replace the CH-46 in the 1990s.

CH-53A/D Sea Stallion An older, less powerful variant of the CH-53E, the Sea Stallion is used by MEBs and MEFs to move cargo and troops.

CH-53E Super Stallion.

CH-53E Super Stallion The CH-53E is the CH-46's big brother. Four of these helicopters are assigned to the ACE of the MEU. Commonly referred to as "Echos," these enormous helicopters are brutes with unrefined strength, but in the hands of their pilots, airborne Echos behave like graceful birds, moving up, down, and sideways quickly, gracefully, and with an agility that would make Cobra pilots envious.

The CH-53E is the essential heavy-lift cargo mover of the MEU and the Marine Corps. Its enormous strength enables it to carry, without any visible difficulty, a suspended load weighing 32,000 pounds (the equivalent of 12 Oldsmobile Cutlasses). It can also carry up to 55 combat-equipped troops. Combat operations today require huge quantities of supplies, and resupply by helicopter is considered essential. Inside, the CH-53E can carry three jeeps, two 105mm howitzers, or seven industrial-sized pallets. With the aid of steel cables suspended from its belly, it can lift almost any aircraft or vehicle in the Marine Corps inventory. It has a range of 450 nautical miles, and if needed, it can refuel in mid-air. Maximum speed is 165 knots, with a cruising speed of 130 knots.

The CH-53E plays a major role in special operations. Its range allows it to come from a long distance beyond the horizon to insert troops, a capability the CH-46 does not have.

129

Close-In Weapon System (CIWS) A computerized gun that can fire off 3,000 rounds per minute.

Combat Rubber Raiding Craft (CRRC) While they look like old-fashioned Zodiac boats, these small rubber crafts are hybrids, equipped with rigid decks that give them much more stability. CRRCs and the new Rigid Raiding Craft give an MEU commander the means to insert troops clandestinely.

Combat Service Support Area (CSSA) A mobile support area that follows the front line of a battle.

Commander, Naval Special Warfare Command (COMNAVSPECWARCOM) The U.S. Navy special operations command, which includes Navy SEALs and a special boat squadron.

Computers The 26th MEU, in particular, demonstrates how well computers simplify planning operations and improve the ability of MEUs to respond to crises rapidly and successfully. Initially, many in the Corps (like many civilians) resisted the use of computers, but under the leadership of Colonel John B. Creel Jr., who commanded the 26th MEU from 1987 to 1990, computers became as essential as standard weapons. Contingency plans for a large number of emergencies are stored in computers. They can be updated quickly, eliminating the often time-consuming manual rework of past contingency plans.

Dog-and-Pony-Show Special operations and training are supposed to be silent, nearly invisible nighttime events. Nevertheless, they attract considerable attention from Congress and the press. Any Marine in a SOC-qualified unit quickly adds to his repertoire the ability to deal with large numbers of official guests. VIP Exercise or VIPEX are other names given to these demonstrations held for visitors.

EA-6B Prowler The sophisticated systems on a Prowler provide MAGTF operations with electronic countermeasure and tactical intelligence support. They are deployed with MEBs and MEFs.

F/A-18 Hornet The Hornet, deployed with MEBs and MEFs, is a lightweight fighter/attack aircraft used by MEBs and MEFs for carrier operations.

Fast Attack Vehicle (FAV) FAVs are Jeeps that have been beefed up with a stronger suspension and roll bar. Three Marines man an FAV, which can carry in a mount either .50-caliber machine guns, M60 machine guns, TOW anti-armor missiles, Dragon missiles, or MK-19 grenade launchers. FAVs may be loaded onto helicopters with all weapons ready. When the helicopter lands on or near an airfield, the Jeeps can drive out, providing instant fire support.

Fast Attack Vehicle mounted with a .50-caliber machine gun.

Fastroping An easy-to-learn skill, however daunting it may appear, fastroping has virtually replaced rappelling as the favorite means to cover the vertical distances between a hovering helicopter and, for

highly sensitive. Snipers, who typically work in teams, have trained themselves to be absolutely still—even a minute movement will throw the round off target. As one sniper fires, a second, acting as an observer, uses a 20-power magnification telescope to view the target and impacts. For night operations, the M40A1 can be equipped with a night-vision scope, which uses moonlight or starlight for target illumination.

M47 Dragon Missile This anti-armor rocket, which can achieve a range of 1,000 meters in 6.2 seconds, can be carried by one Marine and is shoulder-launched.

M60 Medium Battle Tank An older U.S. main battle tank, the M60 is equipped with 105mm cannon, which can be fired at a rate of 6-8 rounds per minute, and a 7.62mm coaxial machine gun. Marine Corps versions were reequipped in the late 1980s with additional armor.

MEUs do not always travel with tanks. It depends on the commander of a given MEU and on the availability of other assets such as Harriers, which some consider "airborne armor" and can, in many missions, make up for the lack of tanks. MEBs and MEBs always travel with tanks.

M60E3 Machine Gun When mounted on a tripod, the M60E3 fires up to 550 7.62mm rounds per minute at a maximum distance of 3,735 meters, with an effective range of 1,100 meters.

Marine Air-Ground Task Force (MAGTF) Since the 1970s the Marine Corps has stressed the MAGTF concept, which provides for combined arms at all levels of Marine unit deployment. These air-ground combat teams are based on existing battalion, regimental, and divisional structures within the Corps. Actual compositions of MAGTFs vary depending on the mission and the availability of Marine units and amphibious shipping. A basic structure appears at right:

Structure

	Marine Expeditionary Unit (MEU)	Marine Expeditionary Brigade (MEB)	Marine Expeditionary Force (MEF)
ground combat element	Battalion Landing Team	Regimental Landing Team	Marine Division
aviation combat element	Reinforced Helicopter Squadron	Reinforced Aircraft Group	Aircraft Wing
combat service support element	MEU Service Support Group	MEB Service Support Group	MEF Service Support Group

Personnel

Marine	2,350	15,000	48,000
Navy	156	670	2,600

Commanded By

	Colonel	Brigadier General	Lieutenant General

Ground Equipment

M-60 Machine Guns	37	89	296
TOW Launchers	8	48	144
AAVs	12	47	208
LAVs	6	36	110
8 inch SP How.	—	—	12
155mm Towed How.	8	24	90
155mm SP How.	—	6	18
81mm Mortars	8	24	72
60mm Mortars	12	27	81
Hawk Launchers	—	6	16
Stinger Teams	5	15	75

Aircraft

AV-8B Harrier	6	40	60
F/A-18 Hornet	—	24	48
A-6 Intruder	—	10	20
EA-6B Prowler	—	4	6
RF-4 Phantom	—	4	8
KC-130 Hercules	2	4	12
OV-10 Bronco	—	6	12
CH-53E Super Stallion	4	8	16
CH-53A/D Sea Stallion	—	20	32
CH-46 Sea Knight	12	48	60
UH-1N Huey	3	12	24
AH-1T/W Cobra	4	12	24

Amphibious Ships

	4–6	21–26	approx. 50

An MEF (I MEF) comprising three MEBs (the First, Fourth, and Seventh) deployed to the Persian Gulf in 1990. Part of its equipment was already in place by the time the MEF deployed; the equipment was located aboard special U.S. Naval Service Maritime Prepositioning Ships.

Marine Amphibious Unit (MAU) These units were renamed Marine Expeditionary Units in 1988.

Marine Expeditionary Brigade (MEB) An air-ground task force that includes about 15,600 Marines and Sailors. The MEB is substantially larger than an MEU, but significantly smaller than a Marine Expeditionary Force. The MEB includes a Regimental Landing Team, Composite Aircraft Group, and MEB Service Support Group

Marine Expeditionary Force (MEF) The largest deployable force of the Marine Corps, comprising a Marine Division, an Aircraft Wing, and a MEF Service Support Group for a combined total of about 50,000 Marines and Sailors.

Marine Expeditionary Unit (MEU) Approximately 2,500 Marines and Sailors make up the MEU, the smallest deployable force of the Marine Corps, which includes a Battalion Landing Team, Composite Aircraft Squadron, and MEU Service Support Group.

MEU Service Support Group (MSSG) The logistics unit that supports an MEU.

Marine Expeditionary Unit, Special Operations Capable (MEU (SOC)) A forward-deployed MEU that has earned the SOC designation after a rigorous six-month predeployment training. Only two MEU (SOC)s are on deployment at any time, one in the Pacific and one in the Mediterranean. After deployment, the MEU loses its SOC designation to a newly trained MEU that is about to deploy.

Maritime Special Purpose Force (MSPF) Contains Marines and Sailors specifically trained to conduct six MEU (SOC) missions.

Mediterranean Amphibious Ready Group (MARG) The U.S. Navy counterpart to a Marine Expeditionary Unit in the Mediterranean.

MK-19 Grenade Launcher This machine-gun-like device fires 40mm grenades at distances of up to 2,200 meters with a maximum effective range of 1,500 meters. The sustained rate of fire is 40 rounds per minute, but the unit can operate at a fast, cyclic rate of 325-375 rounds per minute. This weapon is a prime example of what the Marine Corps has done to beef up the fire power of its infantry units. One MK-19 can lay down a devastating carpet of grenades and requires only two Marines to carry and operate it. At least 25 Marines would be necessary to accomplish the same result with traditional grenade launchers mounted under a rifle. The MK-19 is also being mounted on AAVs, HMMWVs, and FAVs.

Modular Universal Laser Equipment.

Modular Universal Laser Equipment (MULE) Among the most novel items in the Marine Corps' inventory is the Modular Universal Laser Equipment (MULE), a self-contained portable laser designator used for precision-guided munitions such as Hellfire and Copperhead. A spotter relatively close to a target will point the laser designator on a target. "Smart" bombs equipped with guidance mechanisms responsive to the laser that are released from an attack plane, or rounds fired from a howitzer will, in theory and often in practice, land right on the spot illuminated by the laser.

Mortars An efficient and cost-effective weapon, a mortar in a firefight can launch nine pounds of high-explosive rounds, smoke shells, hot-burning white phosphorous rounds, illumination rounds, or air-fuse rounds (that explode in midair just above the impact zone and are designed as anti-troop rounds). The MEU carries two types of mortars: the 60mm and the 81mm.

The 60mm mortar can be found in all four rifle companies, and the 81mm can be found only in the weapons company where other heavy weapons are fielded. Both mortars can be carried by Marines in the field, although the 81mm is much heavier and not truly suited for long-distance marches. The 60mm can fire high-explosive rounds at distances of up to 3,500 meters, white phosphorus rounds at distances of up to 1,650 meters, and illumination rounds at distances of up to 950 meters. The more powerful 81mm mortar can fire substantially heavier (and more lethal) rounds, with a range for high-explosive and white-phosphorus rounds of up to 4,595 meters and illumination rounds of up to 3,350 meters.

MP-5 Submachine Gun Built by Germany's Heckler & Koch, the small MP-5 fires 9mm rounds at up to 350 rounds per minute and is used exclusively by the MEU's Force Reconnaissance Detachment.

MT1XX/MC-4 RAMAIR Parachute The

MP-5 Submachine Gun.

MT1XX/MC-4 RAMAIR parachute allows directional control for steering and has up to 15 knots of forward velocity. Provided wind conditions are right, a deep reconnaissance team could jump some 30 miles away from the intended drop zone and guide themselves to their target, thus reducing the risk of detection by enemy radar.

Night-Vision Goggles (NVGs) Used both in the air and on the ground, NVGs come in a range of models. All work on the same principal: any visible light (such as moonlight and starlight) is electronically amplified to achieve luminance gains of 10.4 to 10.5, thus converting non-visible radiation into a visible display. This process enables NVG wearers to "see in the dark." The image the pilot sees appears green because of the color of the phosphor used on the phosphor viewing screen.

There are currently two types of NVGs in use in the Corps: the AN/PVS-5 and the AN/PVS-6.

Noncombatant Evacuation Operation (NEO) The most likely mission of the 18 missions for which an MEU (SOC) trains. During an NEO, an MEU (SOC) would evacuate civilians from a combat zone or threatening environment, such as their 1990 evacuation of Americans from civil-war-torn Liberia.

Osprey V-22 The Marine Corps hopes to field this innovative aircraft in the 1990s. Designed to take off like a helicopter and fly like a turboprop, the Osprey offers long-range, improved survivability and should replace the CH-46 Sea Knight helicopter as the primary troop assault aircraft. Its long range will enable it to operate in raids and over-the-horizon missions together with the LCAC and the CH-53E Sea Stallion.

OV-10 Bronco The Bronco is a multi-purpose, light-attack aircraft flown to conduct visual aerial reconnaissance missions and limited low-level aerial photography.

Psychological Operations or Psychological Warfare (PsyOps) An organization within the Marine Corps that attempts to exploit the enemy's mental weak points by the use of deceit and cunning.

Radios New devices include the Motorola MX-300, a lightweight, short-distance radio that is highly reliable. Its light weight makes it particularly suitable for raids and clandestine operations. It can be attached to the "RACAL" headset, which allows a Marine to operate the radio and keep his hands free. To encrypt voice communications, the Corps uses devices known as KY-57 and KY-65 to provide relatively secure communications. The PPN-19 is a self-contained, man-portable multiband radar transponder beacon that is compatible with aircraft and naval ships. The KL-43 digital telephone-line encryption system allows forces to send secure messages via telephone lines. The PSC-2 digital communications terminal provides burst transmissions for voice communications. Particularly helpful is the expendable RJS jammer, which weighs just 5.5 pounds and, if necessary, can be discarded after a clandestine raid. It is easily portable and can be brought into an area by small boat or parachute.

Amtracs.

Rapid Response Planning Within six hours of receiving the alert or warning order, Marines must be ready to execute a raid. While a typical raid may be company-sized, it is not uncommon to have raids that make use of several companies and draw on diverse support elements, such as naval gunfire from a nearby destroyer, close air support from a carrier 100 miles away, or the resources of the Marines' own AV-8B Harrier jump jets. Several raids may take place simultaneously, such as a noncombatant evacuation in one area, an airfield seizure (to fly out the civilians) in a second, and a separate attack to take out a radar tower in a third. No matter what the scope of the order, Marine Corps planners have only six hours to get the raid started.

To facilitate the process, planners draw on previously developed contingency plans. Maintaining a large inventory of "off-the-shelf" plans is an essential component of rapid planning. Marine officers during predeployment and later aboard ship spend much of their time working up alternate plans for dealing with specific situations. Plans are rehearsed extensively to refine each aspect of the operation.

Regimental Landing Team (RLT) The ground combat element of a Marine Expeditionary Brigade.

Remotely Piloted Vehicle.

Remotely Piloted Vehicle (RPV) RPVs look like model airplanes. Guided from a control on the ground, they can take off, fly over great distances, and land. They are used as forward observers. The one shown in this book is called "Pioneer." It belongs to the Navy and was launched off the USS *Iowa*. RPVs can stay aloft for several hours and can, with video cameras, observe targets far forward for the *Iowa*'s 16-inch guns. Fiberglass construction, wooden propeller, and small size give the RPV a low radar profile, permitting the unit to remain undetected for long periods of time.

Reverse Osmosis Water Purification Unit (ROWPU) A mobile water purifier and desalinization station.

RF-4 Phantom The RF-4 is the reconnaissance version of the F-4 Phantom all-weather, multi-purpose fighter.

Rigid Raiding Craft (RRC) Rigid Raiding Crafts are modified Boston Whalers that can travel some 40 nautical miles on twin 70-horsepower engines. In a typical Battalion Landing Team, one company is equipped with RRCs so that they can be inserted from over the horizon. The boats are equipped with basic navigational aids and have a low radar profile, allowing for a clandestine approach to a beach.

Rigid Raiders.

Satellite Communications.

Special Operations Command (SOCOM) A designation for U.S. Army special operations. The 1st SOCOM includes the Rangers, Special Forces, Delta Forces, a Psychological Operations group, and the 160th Aviation Group.

Special Operations Forces (SOF) A non-official term for any and all special operations groups within the U.S. armed forces.

Special Operations Training Group (SOTG) A SOTG is located at USMC Camp Lejeune, North Carolina, and at USMC Camp Pendleton, California. They are charged with training all special-operations-capable Marines.

Satellite Communications (SATCOM) While all other radios have had difficulties, SATCOM has always worked. This surprisingly simple, high-tech radio consists of a small antenna, which when pointed roughly in the direction of a satellite, permits communications with locations where line-of-sight radios cannot reach.

Sea Air Land (SEAL) Team A special warfare unit of the U.S. Navy.

Sidewinder Missile A standard air-to-air missile with an infrared homing device.

Sparrowhawk Code name for a task-organized reinforced rifle platoon that is used for heliborne reinforcement of any MEU element. See Bald Eagle.

Special Operations Capable (SOC) The SOC designation is given to a deployed MEU that has just completed six months of exhaustive six-month predeployment training and evaluation. A MEU (SOC) is qualified to undertake 18 missions, from Noncombatant Evacuation Operations to Military Operations in Urban Terrain.

Stinger Missile.

Stinger Missiles Hand-held anti-aircraft missile launcher, which, with an infrared honing device, targets the engines of hostile aircraft. It was used successfully by Afghanistan resistance fighters to shoot down Soviet helicopters.

Tactical Logistics Operation Center (TLOC) A communications center set up at the CSSG that monitors radio communications and tracks the flow of inventory.

Terrain Flight (TERF) A generic term that incorporates low-level flight where pilots follow the contour of the ground to avoid detection by enemy radar.

TOW Anti-Tank Missile **T**ube-launched, **O**ptically-tracked, **W**ire-guided missiles attain speeds of more than 1,000 feet per second in the first ½ second of flight before coasting to the target.

Training in an Urban Environment (TRUE) Marine Special Purpose Force/FBI joint training sessions conducted in urban areas throughout the United States several times a year.

UH-1N Huey Used for multiple missions—troop assault, assault escort, aerial command post—the UH-1N can carry up to six troops with a full combat load. It can also be equipped with weapons such as .50-caliber machine guns and 2.75-inch rockets. Its range is limited to 115 nautical miles; its maximum speed is 120 knots, with a 100-knot cruising speed.

Underway Replenishment (UNREP) Term for a technique used to resupply Navy ships at sea.

VIP Exercise (VIPEX) Demonstrations for official visitors of a Marine Expeditionary Unit's special-operations capabilities. See Dog-and-Pony-Show.

Well Deck A section of an amphibious ship from which smaller craft such as AAVs and LCMs are launched. Amphibious ships conduct a "controlled sinking" by filling their well decks with water, enabling the landing craft within them to float out.

LHA-4 USS *Nassau* well deck.

(Above) Amtrac recovered aboard a Landing Ship, Tank. (Overleaf, pages 142-143) UH-1 helicopter approaching the USS *Nassau*.

ENDNOTES

1. A typical MEU contains about 2,500 Marines and Sailors. Larger units are called Marine Expeditionary Brigades, with a combined total of about 15,600 people, and Marine Expeditionary Forces, with a combined total of about 50,000 people.

2. The official list of MEU attachments reads as follows: Detachment, Radio Battalion; Detachment, Interrogator Translator Team (ITT); Detachment, Force Imagery Interpretation Unit (FIIU); Counterintelligence Sub Team; Terrain Analysis Support Team; Sensor Employment Team; Detachment, Air Naval Gunfire Liaison Company (ANGLICO); Detachment, Marine Air Control Group (MACG); Target Information Officer; Aerial Observer; Detachment, Communication Battalion; Detachment, Force Reconnaissance Company; Detachment, Marine Attack Squadron (VMA); and Detachment, Marine Aerial Refueler Transport Squadron (VMGR).